BE
BETTER
IN BED

BE
BETTER
IN BED

RICHARD MACDONALD

 A GODSFIELD BOOK

Library of Congress Cataloging-in-Publication
Data Available

10 9 8 7 6 5 4 3 2 1

Published in 2000 by
Sterling Publishing Company, Inc.
387 Park Avenue South, New York, N.Y. 10016
© 2000 Godsfield Press
Text © 2000 Richard MacDonald

Richard MacDonald asserts the moral right to
be identified as the author of this work.

Distributed in Canada by Sterling Publishing
c/o Canadian Manda Group, One Atlantic
Avenue, Suite 105, Toronto,
Ontario, Canada M6K 3E7
Distributed in Australia by Capricorn Link
(Australia) Pty Ltd, P O. Box 6651, Baulkham
Hills, Business Centre, NSW 2153, Australia

Printed and bound in Hong Kong

Sterling ISBN 0–8069–2771–2

contents

introduction

How to behave in bed? Surely it is obvious, isn't it? Well, no. There are many areas of bedroom manners that are never spoken about openly. This can result in confusion, embarrassment, and awkwardness for one or both partners. For instance, whose job is it to provide the kleenexes or make sure that there are enough condoms? And where do you draw the line when it comes to being asked for new sexual experiences? And, more importantly, how do you draw the line? How do you turn down your lover without causing a major argument?

Setting boundaries and rules

This is a book about setting the boundaries and rules for bedroom behavior so that you are free to enjoy one another. It is about the simple good manners of sex – and how that works for both men and women. But it is about more than that, it is about etiquette; how to behave toward each other as a couple, how you should show your respect for one another, and how you exercise the dignity toward each other that you are both entitled to. Etiquette is not about being prim and proper but about being honorable. It is

Pleasing each other in bed is about personal preferences. Be as bold and as bad as you both want to be.

about thinking of your lover as someone who deserves the very best treatment, the very best sex, and the very best standards of hygiene and personal behavior.

The book is divided into three sections: "Loving Sex for Couples," "Mainly for Men," and "Mainly for Women." It looks at what each of you is individually responsible for in the bedroom first, and then the shared responsibilities and possible hindrances to lovemaking. Feel free to read this book together, although it may be best if you start by reading the relevant sections yourself. It may also be a good idea for you to read the whole book because you will gather further insights into your partner if you read the section aimed at them.

There are examples and suggestions throughout the book. Please feel free to use or discard these as you wish – they are there to inspire, not restrict, you. And they are certainly not there to make you feel bad if you are not doing them all.

Take this book to bed with you and discover the very best in each other.

Everyone is different and some of the subjects covered in this book may not be relevant to your sex life.

What you take from this book is up to you. There may be just one thing that makes an impression on you but will totally transform your sex life. Or the book may just confirm what you have both already been doing. The most important thing to remember is that it is vital for you, as you read the following pages, to honestly consider and review what your bedroom manners are like. Never assume that you know how the other person feels – always ask. Now that's good manners.

PART ONE

LOVING SEX
for couples

All couples evolve their own set of rules and guidelines for bedroom manners. You need to look together at how you behave toward one another in the bedroom, in order to avoid the loss of dignity that can occur when standards are allowed to slip over time.

Making an effort

When you first met your lover, you probably behaved impeccably, treated them with consideration and respect, wined and dined them, and took time and trouble over your personal hygiene and appearance. But after a while these things are allowed to slip, and you can forget that you are both sharing a very intimate and personal space with someone to whom you owe the highest esteem. You must learn to return to that initial approach – one of respect.

Finding out what is acceptable – and what isn't

As a couple you have to work out what is acceptable and what isn't. There are no guaranteed formulas – within each couple what will work for one partner won't necessarily work for the other. The only way to find out what is acceptable behavior is to talk about it, discuss your different wishes and needs, and set an agenda that encompasses both.

Treat each other with consideration and tenderness.

Breaching someone's personal set of guidelines is a sign of disrespect and can signal the failing of a relationship. If you love and care about your partner, it makes sense to maintain good manners in the bedroom. This doesn't mean you have to be stuffy or serious, merely courteous – you can lighten up but still preserve the dignity of your partner as well as yourself.

Good sex is also about having fun – with dignity of course.

This section looks at ways to improve and expand your sexual relationship with your partner while being both romantic and sexy at all times.

WHO IS
responsible for what?

As a couple, you are both responsible for your own actions and the results of those actions. But you have to bear in mind that in any sexual matter you are dealing with another person who, like you, will have doubts, fears, insecurities, and worries. If you praise good performance it's much more likely to be repeated or improved upon

Your job is to support each other. Both partners are responsible for each other's sexual fulfillment.

than if you criticize or deride. Compliments will get you places that insults never will.

If you flatter each other, support each other, love, and are intimate with each other then sex becomes an extension of that love rather than an excuse for it. The term "making love" isn't very accurate; it should be "what is made by the love." You can't have great sex without respect. You can't have respect unless you set boundaries. You have to be responsible. If you don't want one partner to fool around with other people, then you have to take on board some responsibility for their sexuality. If you aren't providing full and satisfying sex, then they may end up looking elsewhere for that satisfaction. It's your job to make sure that they are enjoying a full and varied sex life – just as it is their job to do the same for you.

IGNORE YOUR PARTNER'S NEEDS AT YOUR PERIL

If one of you takes the responsibility for always being the one to initiate sex that's fine as long as both of you have decided that. If, however, this

happened due to a sort of random deselection process it means that one of you is abdicating responsibility. Likewise, where and when sex takes place must be mutually agreed upon and not left to one person to always decide or suggest. The type of sex you have – ranging from the raunchy to the extremely gentle and intimate – needs mutual agreement. If one of you is having the sort of sex they want but the other isn't then the relationship will flounder – and often the introduction of a third person will be the rock that sinks the ship. So often the half of a couple who has been having great sex while ignoring their partner's needs will look confused and not understand when this happens. They may say "I don't know why they went off with X, we were having such a great sex life." But in truth, they weren't because they didn't pay attention to their partner's needs. You must both be having a great sex life for it to be really great.

Having great sex is only half the battle – you and your partner have to have great rapport.

Realize that you're not going to get it right every time, so don't worry – relax and enjoy practicing and experimenting.

GETTING IT RIGHT AND GETTING IT WRONG

The individual details of who is responsible for what (such as condoms and tissues) will be looked at in later sections. But there are bigger responsibilities – love, intimacy, and the "spark" of sex. Sex is an art that needs to be practiced, thought about, talked about, even rehearsed occasionally. You aren't going to get it right every single time and you need to have prepared yourselves collectively for failure, low libido, and the physical impossibility of sex at times – such as just after childbirth or through illness or post-operative recovery.

CHANGING PREFERENCES

You need to have prepared yourselves for the changing sexual preferences and needs that you and your partner will have during your relationship. At

the beginning you may have one sort of sex but a long way down the line when you have been married or living together for many years you may well need a different kind of sex. In fact, the sex will have evolved and changed quite naturally anyway. It's no good one of you hanging onto the romantic ideal of when you first met and were new to it all. Sex changes and you have to change with it. Likewise one of you may have a particular fantasy you want to play out. Once played out it may well be enjoyable but it will no longer have the intrigue of strangeness. Whose responsibility will it be to say that you have had enough of that particular experience and want to try something else? You must be open enough to talk these things through. Never assume you know how or what the other person thinks and feels. Instead, discuss rather than assume, ask – don't demand, encourage rather than damn, and support rather than isolate.

Dos

Do decide jointly between you who is
responsible for what – and stick to it.

✓

Do take your responsibilities
seriously – especially for the big stuff.

✓

Do be responsible for your own actions
and be aware of the repercussions.

Don'ts

Don't assume but discuss.

✗

Don't be lazy or apathetic; rather
be inventive and surprising.

✗

Don't apportion blame – praise success.

WHO SETS THE
sexual agenda?

Who sets the sexual agenda in your relationship, and why? Or have you jointly and cooperatively decided it? Unlikely. Most couples' sex life takes on a "corporate" identity all of its own during the life of the relationship and often neither of the couple is really happy with it nor satisfied by it. This isn't about mismatched libido (*see pages 18–21*) but about the tone and style of the sexual agenda rather than the frequency or availability of it.

Never be judgmental about what your partner wants – what's on the sexual agenda should be a joint decision.

What sort of a sex life do you want individually? What sort of a sex life do you think your partner wants? What sort of "corporate" sex life have you both got? Do you both want this? Are you both happy with this? What can you change? What would you change?

BEING JUDGMENTAL

All these questions need answering if you are to approach your sex life with good grace, good manners, and good etiquette. You must not assume that what you want from your sex life is the same as what your partner wants. And never assume that whoever it is that is setting the sexual agenda is the right person. Everything needs to be clarified and checked. For instance, you have to look at what is going on in your sex life. This could be anything from gentle lovemaking in bed in the nude once a week, to sado-masochism clubs, other people involved, sex outdoors, raunchy sex, role playing, sex toys and aids, transvestitism, teasing, flaunting,

voyeurism, and pornography. Before you begin discounting any of these you have to take what your partner wants into consideration.

You cannot enter into a sexual agenda with prior judgments. What your partner wants is as important as what you want and you cannot be judgmental when it comes to another person's sexuality. The best way forward into a truly liberated and happy sex life is compromise. If one of you only wants gentle lovemaking and the other wants to join a swinger's club then you will have to find a way for both of you to get what you want while still maintaining a healthy and stable relationship. Obviously if the two wants and needs are so completely at odds then you will have to question why you're in a relationship with someone with whom you share so little in common. Are you prepared to compromise to keep your relationship alive?

What your partner wants is important – learn to talk to each other and reach compromises about each other's sexual needs.

SETTING THE AGENDA

Most couples evolve a sexual agenda without giving it any thought or planning – it just sort of evolves organically. Often when this happens one partner is unhappy or unsatisfied and isn't saying so. You have to jointly decide – and it must be a conscious decision – what sort of sexual people you are. You have to decide what turns you on and off, what you like and dislike, and what you need for satisfaction and don't need. And of course you have to consider what your partner needs. You have to take responsibility for each other's sexuality. It's your job as a lover to make sure that your partner is getting the right sort of sex to empower them in all other facets of their life – and that might mean you compromising, suspending your own judgments and preferences occasionally, not being shocked or horrified, being considerate, and being magnanimous. If you're not being all this what are you being? If you're not helping your lover find sexual satisfaction how are you helping? If you're not allowing and empowering your lover sexually then what are you doing?

Setting a sexual agenda and taking your partner's needs into consideration doesn't mean sex should be routine. Even planned sex should be fun – as well as safe and spontaneous.

BEING KIND TO EACH OTHER

This doesn't mean sex has to be clinical or planned, all thought out and serious. It can still be fun, spontaneous, raunchy, loving, gentle, intimate, reassuring, and safe. All you have to do is jointly decide on what sort of sex you both need and make compromises, deal kindly with each other's desires and needs, be supportive, and be open to your partner's sexuality. You could also try taking turns to choose. Suppose for one week or on one liaison one of you decides and then the other can be "in charge" on the next occasion.

Dos

Do discuss what needs you both have.

✓

Do be responsible for your partner's
sexual satisfaction and enjoyment.

✓

Do take turns in choosing what sort
of sex you are going to have.

Don'ts

Don't let your sex life evolve without thought.

✗

Don't allow your sexual agenda to be based on
assumptions or guesswork – ask and discuss.

WHAT ABOUT
mismatched libido?

We all get turned off of sex from time to time. We get tired, sick, need to recover from surgery or childbirth, get stressed to the point where our performance and libido are affected adversely – and sometimes we just can't be bothered. This isn't a problem if you live alone or aren't in a relationship. But when you are half of a couple then

Stress can affect your sex drive – be open with your partner about how you feel, instead of bottling things up.

what affects you also affects your lover. You can't have good sex in isolation – you need your partner.

SHARING A PROBLEM

If one of you wants to abstain, but the other doesn't, then someone is going to feel unsatisfied with your sex life. Perhaps the one who doesn't feel like it is being pressured into going through with it, and is feeling bad about that. Or maybe the one who wants to isn't having any sex at all, and is upset by that. Either way one, or even both, of you will be feeling bad. If either you or your partner are feeling like this then there's a problem. And what is a problem for one becomes, by nature of the fact it's a relationship, a problem for both of you. If it's not a problem for you then clearly your partner's sexuality isn't an important item on your personal agenda. You must question yourself, and possibly the validity of the relationship.

But if you are happy with the fundamentals of your relationship and are both in love with each other then your partner's sex life has to be of some importance to you. And this isn't about how often but is also about the type of sex (*see pages 32–35*).

If you are the one who doesn't feel like having sex, for whatever reason, and your partner still wants and needs regular sex, you have a duty not to neglect their needs. Although you may not feel like full penetrative sex you can still offer caressing, fondling, masturbation, and oral sex. Their need is still to be satisfied and to be physically in touch. Your need may be for these things not to happen for a while. You have to seek compromise. If you see sex on a scale of 0 to 10 and you want 0 then obviously your partner can't expect to have 10 – but you could offer 1 or 2 rather than hope your partner will be satisfied with coming down to your 0 – they won't. Be considerate of your partner's physical capacity for sex – they may not be as active as you and likewise they will be considerate of your needs and desires.

At certain times, differing sex drives mean we need to change the way we make love – perhaps because of pregnancy.

BEING PATIENT AND SUPPORTIVE

If you're the one who is still sexually active and lusty and it's your partner who has the low libido, for whatever reason, then it's your job to be kind and considerate, and to temper your needs with those of your lover's. Even if they are "off" sex for the moment they still love you and you must be patient and supportive. If you seek 10 on the scale and they feel like 0 then you must be prepared to accept 1 or 2 for the time being. This might mean accepting an intimate fondle while you masturbate. The important thing is not to be demanding, sulky, or ill-tempered. If you are supportive, caring, kind, and understanding then it's likely that your partner will feel like sex again a lot more quickly than if you pressure them or threaten to seek sex elsewhere.

REASONS FOR LOW LIBIDO

Low libido is not just a temporary state caused by external factors such as tiredness or ill health. If the spark has gone from your relationship and the love is dead then libido will be low and no amount of techniques or sex manuals can solve the problem. But you must also remember that in any long-term stable relationship there will be times when you are both more, or less, in love with each other. Give these times a little space and the feelings will usually restore themselves – as long as there is no obligation to have sex.

Sometimes there may even be a medical reason for low libido so a visit to a medical practitioner is advisable. Some forms of alternative medicine, such as Traditional Chinese Medicine, report good results in treating this condition. But really the best treatment is time and care. The more the spotlight is thrown on low libido the more of a problem it can become but with gentle consideration and patience it usually resolves itself.

Be supportive at all times and allow your partner the freedom to say "no."

Dos

Do accept that in all relationships there are
times of low libido.

✓

Do give each other time and patience
if there is a temporary low libido.

✓

Do seek guidance and advice
if the problem is ongoing.

Don'ts

Don't pressure or bully your partner
into doing anything they don't want to.

HOW TO HAVE SEX WITHOUT
offending the neighbors

Make love in the backyard if you want to – but make sure your neighbors can't hear.

Your sex life is a continual, constantly evolving, ever-changing activity that needs to be revitalized, pepped up, spiced up, kept active, and generally maintained. And all this needs to be done within the boundaries of good etiquette. So before you embark on a new and exciting version of "postman's knock" do take your immediate neighbors into consideration.

They may not care to lie awake listening to you and your lover having wild and raunchy sex on the hood of your car in the front drive or catch a naked glimpse of you as you chase each other around the backyard. Be circumspect. You don't have to curtail your fun – just be a little discreet. Taking others into consideration is good manners.

FINDING THE RIGHT SPACE

The same goes for having sex outdoors – choose your place carefully and don't offend people. You can still have lots of fun and be as free as you like. Just be aware that what you consider spicy may be viewed by others as extreme and shocking. You don't want to ruin a good relationship with your neighbors, and they probably don't want to share your most intimate moments, so use your initiative. It doesn't take too much hunting around to find a suitable place – and this can then become a favorite part of spicing up your sex life. Check out your local laws for what you can get away with – and what you can't.

Have lots of fun outdoors – but be discreet and take others' feelings into consideration.

Dos

Do be aware that your sex life needs
constant updating to keep it fresh.

✓

Do be willing to experiment and try new things.

✓

Do keep the noise down during late hours.

Don'ts

Don't shock or offend your neighbors.

✗

Don't get caught.

✗

Don't forget to have fun.

HOW TO HAVE SEX AND CHILDREN
at the same time

Sex is a wonderful activity with a fantastic bonus – it produces children. Unfortunately, when they do come along sex often takes a bit of a back seat as we all get tired, stressed, busy, and pressured. When this happens, if you neglect the physical side of your relationship, then, the whole relationship can become threatened. It is important to maintain a full and active sex life, if you want to keep the intimacy and closeness with your partner. And remember that your children will feel much more secure if they can see how much their parents love each other.

Keep your children's toys and your own toys separate.

LEARNING WHEN TO BE SELFISH

Children can present problems because they do demand so much of parents that there sometimes seems little left over – but you must be selfish occasionally if you want to retain your sanity and a good relationship with your partner. For instance, it is okay to have set bedtimes for children and make them stick to them, so you can have the evenings to yourselves – even if that means just watching television or catching up on the papers, or, of course, having sex. There is also nothing wrong with children learning respect for other people's privacy. Your children can be taught to knock before entering their parents' bedroom so that you can enjoy yourselves safe in the knowledge that you will get a little warning before they burst in on you. You can also opt for a four-poster bed, or one that is screened, for extra privacy. If you teach children to knock first before entering it is only fair that you knock before entering their room.

HIDING THE EVIDENCE

Make sure you put away anything you use as part of your sex life such as vibrators, condoms, lubricating jelly, handcuffs, or erotic pictures so that if your children come into your room they will not ask embarrassing or awkward questions. And as teenagers they will not expect or want you to have a sex life and would prefer not to even think about it so don't force them to – be discreet!

Once young children have gone to bed at night the house is yours to enjoy as you would want to but you should still watch noise levels. There is nothing more worrying to a small child than hearing its parents make love without knowing what is going on. You can always use a baby monitor to check whether they are asleep or not before indulging your passions – perhaps you might relax more if you know they are asleep.

Indulge your passions – but tidy up afterward if you want to avoid any awkward questions from your little ones.

BE DISCREET BUT AFFECTIONATE

While you should keep your sex life discreet and away from your children, you should allow them to see that you are in love. Let them see you kissing, holding hands, hugging, and caressing as long as nothing goes too far. It is a good role model for children to see their parents in love and being loving. They will grow up much more affectionate and will find it easier to be physical if they have seen it happening in their own family life.

Whether you let your children see you in the nude is entirely up to you. Young children don't seem to mind and are usually quite fascinated by nudity. This fascination does wear off with time and teenagers will appreciate it more if they don't ever see you naked. Men might like to give due consideration to their erections, especially first thing in the morning – is it healthy for your children to see them? You have to make your own decisions as to this sort of thing but discretion should be your key word in all matters.

TAKING TIME OFF

There are times when one or other of you will be unable to have sex – immediately after childbirth, for instance, or if the man has just had a vasectomy. It is at these times that having children and sex simply aren't compatible. But a normal and healthy sex life can and should be resumed as soon as possible. The exact timing of this must be decided jointly. There must be no pressure to start sex again until you have both fully recovered physically and emotionally. Talk to each other about when to resume.

Children are exhausting but they shouldn't interfere with your sex life – you just have to be smart in how you arrange your time and priorities.

Letting your children see you in love and being affectionate with each other is a good thing.

Dos

Do make time for each other.

✓

Do keep the noise down.

✓

Do have a set routine for children – and stick to it.

✓

Do show your children that you love each other.

Don'ts

Don't forget to keep your sex life discreet – especially from teenagers who are easily embarrassed.

✗

Don't allow having children to adversely affect your sex life – make the time to enjoy each other.

✗

Don't hesitate to have privacy and respect in the bedroom.

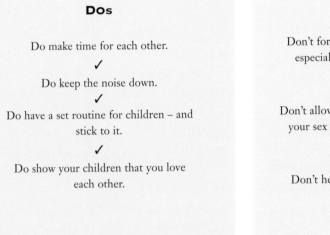

LOVE

LOVE
games

When you aren't actually making love you may be playing love games that lead to sex. These can vary from chasing each other around the house in the nude to quite complicated games of role playing and dressing up. The etiquette of such games is important if you want to continue to play them in safety and trust.

Don't play sex games with a new lover – only established partners know where to draw the line.

SAYING "STOP" AND MEANING IT

Perhaps you and your lover like to play out mild fantasies such as being tied up and titillated. That is fine as long as both of you know the boundaries, and know where to draw the line between acting out fantasies and them becoming real and scary. For instance you should have a key word that, when said, means "stop" and you both stop no matter what. Sex games should only happen within a stable and loving relationship because using such a key word has to be based on mutual respect and trust. You simply don't get these with a stranger during casual sex. It is much better to play in safety with your long-term lover than to take unnecessary risks.

Love games can take many forms depending on the couple and their sexual inclinations, and the etiquette of such games may well be based on habits built up over many years. For instance, you may well like making love outdoors and pretending to be on safari or camped in the desert. The etiquette for this might be that it only happens when both of you feel it is warm, secluded, and safe enough.

Love games can include anything you want. Enjoy sharing food in the nude – and licking off any spillages.

If one of you is unsure the other should be respectful and take a raincheck on that game.

UNSPOKEN RULES

You might have a game of playing rude touching in shopping malls and seeing how much you can get away with. The etiquette of this game might be that you only play it in places where you are sure you won't bump into anyone you know – or be seen by the children's teacher. If you both subscribe to the etiquette it will work well. You only get problems when one partner won't play fair or the etiquette

Pretend to be on safari or camped in the desert and see what happens.

isn't clearly laid down at the start.
Unspoken rules often present the greatest
problems since you both assume you know
the rules but you may well have interpreted
them differently. You won't notice this until
there is a clear infringement of the rules
and you are both working from a different
set of guidelines. Set out the rules verbally so that
there can be no misunderstanding at a later date.
Be specific about what you are playing and how
to stop it if either of you want to.

Set out the rules
before you begin
love games to
avoid any
misunderstanding.

The etiquette of love games is always to
remember that that is exactly what they are –
games. They should be fun and enjoyable
and if at any moment they become scary
they should be stopped at once. Love games
need an air of safety and confidence built
around them. It is no good starting a game
when you know your in-laws are about to
arrive or the children could walk in on you. And
you should only begin when you feel safe and
reassured about the game that is about to be played.

MUTUAL LOVE GAMES

Love games should also be
mutual. That doesn't mean you
must both design them or suggest
them, merely that you both must want
to play and be prepared to participate
fully. If the game is exclusively your
partner's then you must take turns
and they should allow you a
chance to play games of your own.

DOS

Do play games – your sex
life shouldn't be all serious.

✓

Do set boundaries and guidelines
before you play love games.

✓

Do jointly agree a key word
to mean "stop" and stick to it.

✓

Do allow your partner the right of veto.

✓

Do engender an atmosphere
of trust in which to play games.

DON'TS

Don't play one partner's games
exclusively but take turns.

✗

Don't let love games get out of hand or out of
control – maintain decorum and good etiquette
even in the heat of passion.

✗

Don't get stuck in a rut – vary
love games and be inventive.

HOW TO ASK FOR
new experiences

Sex is an ongoing experience that is subject to change over the years. If you want to keep it fresh, vibrant, and exciting then you have to evolve with it. You have to maintain interest and intrigue. If you allow sex to become boring or routine it will trail off and the relationship will become defective. By introducing new things into your sex life – and letting go of them again when they too become boring – you will keep your sex life fresh. But how do you go about asking for new things without appearing to be saying that you think things are too staid and dull?

Spice things up with sexy toys – but only if you both agree.

A WILLING ACCOMPLICE

Well, hopefully, you will have developed a sexual agenda together that will be based on mutual respect and trust, and will have already tried some experimentation. You should both know each other pretty well and know what sort of things are going to be rejected or accepted. Your partner should be your willing accomplice in all matters sexual so you should already have a clear idea of where the boundaries are (*see page 40–43*). If you don't then you haven't been doing your homework.

If you know your partner absolutely hates wasting food or creating a mess then there is probably not a lot of point suggesting bathing in baked beans or smearing each other's genitalia in honey or

Be romantic and dress to please your lover – and undress, of course!

cream. If you know your partner has a history of sea sickness then suggesting making love in a small rowboat on a moonlit lake might be romantic to you but bad manners to them. Be circumspect and do a little research before hand.

YOU WANT TO DO WHAT?!

Don't ask for anything that you know will shock your partner and don't ask for anything that is seriously unhealthy, dangerous, illegal, causes permanent damage, or is likely to be a threat to the relationship – and this last one includes involving other people. You might like the idea of joining a swinger's club and are pretty sure you can get

When trying out new experiences, know where the boundaries are and stick to them.

your partner's cooperation, albeit reluctantly, but it's going to end in disaster unless they are 100 percent behind the idea in the first place. Good sex is based on love and respect so don't ask for anything of each other that could jeopardize either of those. Even the raunchiest of sex should still be enjoyed in an atmosphere of love and mutual esteem. Don't ask for anything that seems to indicate abuse, humiliation, or contempt of the other's gender as this could affect the whole relationship. Don't be afraid to say "no."

CRAVING INDULGENCES

Within these reasonable confines you can still ask for pretty well anything you want to do or have never tried and your partner should be open and free enough to consider any sexual activity without instantly dismissing your suggestions and ideas. Each person's sexuality is unique and entirely their own business. If you want your partner to wash you in custard and lock you in the closet then they ought to be indulgent enough to try it rather than just laugh at you. However you also ought to be aware before you ask that they probably will laugh. Question the humor or validity of what you are asking for before you do the asking. Ideally asking for new experiences should be done in

the atmosphere of a discussion so that you can feel part of a couple that is seeking out new experiences rather than a selfish individual. Instead of having to say "I would like to…" you can jointly explore a subject and say "have we ever tried…"And then decide together whether you want to or not. How much you discuss what you are prepared to try or want to experiment with as a couple is a good and healthy indication of how open and relaxed you are with each other.

"Pour me a custard bath darling!" Whatever you want is fine – just ask.

Dos

Do feel free to discuss
new ideas with your partner.

✓

Do be inventive and stimulating.

✓

Do take the opportunity to explore your
sexuality together in a spirit of trust and respect.

Don'ts

Don't expect your partner to go along
with anything that would be unhealthy
to the relationship.

✗

Don't shock your partner – be cautious when
suggesting anything completely new.

✗

Don't dismiss your partner's suggestions
without considering them first.

✗

Don't explore areas that you
know your partner doesn't want to.

HOW TO REFUSE

new experiences

What if you are asked to do something you don't want to do? How do you reject your partner's suggestions without seemingly rejecting them as well? You must learn to treat them with respect but be honest enough to tell them if you are not happy with their suggestions. But at the same time you should be open enough to try just about anything if they want you to.

Don't throw out any good ideas before you have suggested them to your partner.

SECRET SEXUAL AGENDAS

Each of us has a secret sexual agenda consisting of things we'd really like to do but have never dared to, or have never had the opportunity to do. That secret agenda is very private and very vulnerable. None of us wants to be seen as depraved, corrupt, or sinful but we do harbor urges and desires that we might like to act out. Suggesting yours to your partner requires a lot of trust and confidence. You know you might be rejected but hopefully you feel safe enough to accept this.

If you get asked to do something you really don't want to do, you should be aware of how fragile your partner's sexual esteem might be and be flattered that they feel open enough to ask anyway. Never reject your partner's sexual needs without thinking – that is simply not fair or courteous. If you don't want to have anything to do with what they are suggesting it is kinder to say, "you'll have to give me some time to think about that – but we could try…" and then suggest a compromise, a moderated version, or even something completely different. Just saying "Urgh, no, that's a revolting suggestion" will leave your partner feeling rejected, hurt, and humiliated. Find a kind way of saying no.

BEING OPEN TO NEW EXPERIENCES

You should set boundaries together (*see pages 40–43*) fairly early on in any relationship so that you both know what is acceptable and what isn't. This doesn't mean that you can't be open to new experiences suggested by one of you, it just gives you a basis of trust and a knowledge of what the other person is prepared to do.

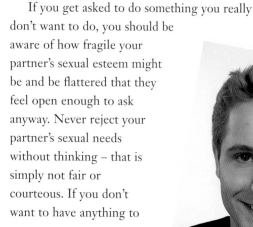

Say "no" if you don't like your partner's suggestion – but say it in a friendly way.

Set the rules together for new experiences and be prepared to compromise.

SAYING "NO" AND SAYING WHY

If there is something you feel strongly about and simply don't want to do then say so firmly (but kindly) and stick to it. If you feel something is fundamentally unhealthy toward you or the relationship you have to be firm and resolute. Don't be persuaded by the power of argument or the threat of pouting. Don't cave in to pressure. State your grounds and stick to them. If your partner wants to have a threesome but you know this will damage the relationship then say no and say why. If your partner wants to do something to you that you feel is unwise, unhealthy, or is likely to cause you regret then say so and again say why. No one should be bullied into anything they don't want to do.

Be polite when you turn down suggestions. Remember that you are rejecting your partner's ideas, not them. If you are genuinely shocked by an idea you can say so – but remember it is the idea that you find shocking, not your partner. Saying, "I don't think I could do that because…" is fine, but saying, "I couldn't do that and I'm disgusted with you for even suggesting it," really isn't helpful. If you handle rejecting a suggestion badly your partner will be much more reticent about suggesting anything in the future, so you will have killed a source of inspiration and creativity that could have done wonders for your sex life later. Think ahead and don't cut off your nose to spite your partner.

We do all occasionally push it and ask for something we know is repulsive or unexciting to our partner. It's as if we like to play around with rejection. So if you always say yes, when your partner is unfairly pushing it you will find it much harder to say no. Remember that saying no firmly is fine as long as it is done politely.

Don't push it if you know your partner has said "no," especially if they have let you down gently.

DOS

Do say no firmly but politely
if you don't want to do something.

✓

Do set your boundaries and stick to them.

✓

Do take your partner's feelings
into consideration when rejecting an idea.

DON'TS

Don't do anything you don't want to
but do consider suggestions first.

✗

Don't let your sex life become stale or dull.

✗

Don't suggest things you know your partner
will feel uncomfortable with.

✗

Don't sulk or become aggressive if your partner
says no to your suggestion.

boundaries and rules

In any interaction between two people there has to be boundaries and rules – even if it is only a casual business transaction such as buying a newspaper. Within a loving, sexual relationship these rules and boundaries are extremely important because they form the basis of trust and respect upon which the entire relationship is based. If you want to have a successful, rich, and rewarding relationship then you have to have your personal boundaries respected. This means, quite simply, that your partner knows what you like and dislike in the way of bedroom etiquette, you know their wishes, and you are both considerate enough not to breach these boundaries.

Set the sexual rules by having a clear cut way of saying "no."

ACCEPTING THE INEVITABLE

You can't change a person's personality but you can get them to change their behavior. For instance, if your partner is very messy and you are very neat it might drive you crazy; you are always straightening up and they are always making a mess; you put your clothes away neatly and they drop theirs on the floor. You can't turn them into a neat person overnight – but you can get them to change their behavior. By giving them something to put their clothes on, they may drop them on the floor less often; by arranging a suitable closet with lots of space, you may get a tidier bedroom; accepting that they and you don't share the same neatness regime might make you a little less stressed by the situation. If you constantly strive to change their personality then you are doomed to failure and frustration. If, on the other hand, you accept the inevitable and plan accordingly and cleverly you have a greater chance of success.

CLEARING UP MISUNDERSTANDINGS

Rules and boundaries should be jointly worked out and you don't have to have the same rules, they can be different for each of you. Setting boundaries often occurs spontaneously within a relationship. There is room for mistaken assumptions and a corporate set of rules that neither of you is really happy with. By taking some time to discuss them together, you are likely to clear up any seed of misunderstanding before it takes root. You will find that doing this generates true intimacy and respect.

THE BIG STUFF

So what sort of boundaries and rules do you need? Well, that varies from relationship to relationship but you could consider the big questions first: Will you tolerate each other having affairs (and don't assume that just because you don't want to or think your partner

Don't wait until you're making love to lay down rules and guidelines.

doesn't want to means that they think or feel the same), how far are you prepared to go sexually, do you want children, how much love and respect are you prepared to give each other (and it does vary from relationship to relationship), who is responsible for what when it comes to bedroom etiquette, and what are your long-term goals for you, the relationship, and your partner? These are the sort of issues that cause a lot of relationships to flounder just because they have never been discussed so each partner assumes they know how the other thinks and feels. When it all goes horribly wrong they are left confused – don't let your relationship end like that. You owe it to each other to be clear.

THE REALLY BIG STUFF

You will need rules about honesty and trust – for example, if one partner asks the other if a particular outfit is cool or classy and the other tells the truth is this okay? And how much truth are you entitled to? Do you really want an honest opinion of what your partner thinks about your mother – or should there be a little tolerance and tact? You decide, they're your rules after all. Or rather they're both of yours, so make sure you discuss all of these sticky issues together. And make sure that you both feel open enough to discuss these matters calmly and without criticism.

Honesty and trust are the basis for a good relationship. But you should both decide if you prefer brutal honesty or tact.

THE LITTLE STUFF

You also need rules about privacy and personal space, bathroom etiquette, silly things like bed making, whose job it is to throw away the old newspapers from the bedroom, and who is responsible for the crumbs under the sheets. You definitely need rules for personal hygiene (*see pages 76–79 and 110–13*) and whether you will cut toenails in front of each other – that sort of thing.

Dos

Do discuss rules and personal boundaries
early on in a relationship if possible.

✓

Do expect that both of you will keep to them.

✓

Do discuss any misunderstandings
rather than brood on them.

Don'ts

Don't violate your partner's rules and
personal boundaries, particularly if they
are different from yours.

✗

Don't allow mistaken assumptions to go on
being made – talk about them openly.

HOW TO BE
intimate with one another

We have different
expectations of what a
relationship means.

A frequent cause of relationship failure is a mismatched expectation of what we want, and get, from our partners. In general terms women complain of a lack of intimacy and romance and men complain of a lack of raunchy sex and frivolity. While these two issues may not seem to be related they do in fact stem from the same root. We all need to be loved and want our lover to express that love in a tangible and recognizable form. For men this means in sex and for women this means tenderness – generally speaking of course.

Men often complain that the sex has tailed off and yet they do nothing to restore the feelings of warmth and intimacy (*see pages 84–87*). Women complain that the intimacy has gone but do nothing to generate it by restoring the declining sexual activity. There is usually much room for compromise on both sides.

EXCESS EMOTIONAL BAGGAGE

The secret of intimacy is simple – if you demand it, it won't happen. However, if you engineer it, it is much more likely to happen. You could communicate with your partner that you feel sexually uninterested when they only touch you sexually in bed at the end of the day. We could explain that if they were to touch us much more romantically and intimately during the day then it would generate a more physical response. But most of us don't. Instead, we carry excess emotional baggage merely because we don't communicate our needs or make the effort to compromise. If you don't talk, your partner can't hear what you want.

The secret of a good relationship is caring deeply for each other. This means that you must care enough to listen when your partner brings up a problem. You must try to overcome it, even if it isn't a problem for you. Remember that if it's a problem for one of you then it is a problem for both. A lack of intimacy, for whichever partner, is a problem you should both be aware of – in a good caring relationship it can be dealt with successfully. By explaining what you need you stand a better chance of getting it than if you bottle it up and do not express yourself. And sometimes that is all a problem needs – expression. By simply saying that you feel ignored or unromanced you can engineer change if your partner is sufficiently caring. The etiquette is in choosing your moment and the style of communication. Demanding, sulking, harassing, or withholding favors are all methods guaranteed to fail. Talking in a calm and kind way is better – it gets results – and don't forget you need to compromise as well as your partner.

Be expressive at all times – say what you feel. By being in tune with each other's needs, you will achieve true intimacy.

EXPRESSING YOUR WANTS

When you express your wants you must be prepared to listen to your partner's in return – that's the basis of good communication. It is no good merely telling them what you want and not offering anything in return. And no, this doesn't mean surrendering your personal rights, it merely means accepting compromise and being adult

about your wants and needs. You have to realize that you are dealing not only with another person but with another sex entirely and they may or may not understand what it is you need. Obviously you know your partner better than anyone else and you are in the best position to judge how responsive they are to you. Both sexes can usually eventually see when a lack of intimacy is a problem and should be able to do something about it. What men find difficult to understand are vague demands such as "talk to me" or "we aren't close enough" so women need to be specific and clear when communicating. Men need to realize that women aren't just funny sorts of men with breasts but a separate type of human being altogether. Men have to be prepared to spend time with their partner in the way they want. And that's time being intimate and romantic. The solution is with the men, they have to open up and share their feelings – and they do have them too!

We all need to be loved and to be touched gently and romantically; we all need to be wined and dined, seduced, and cared about; we all need to be treated respectfully and with tenderness. The etiquette of intimacy is to be able to generate these things without using a confrontational demand. Express yourself clearly and kindly.

Be prepared to listen – what your partner is saying is important.

Dos

Do express your needs
and wants clearly and gently.

✓

Do have a high expectation of what
a relationship should be in intimate terms.

✓

Do make sure you give your partner the space to
express their needs and wants as well.

✓

Do be prepared to compromise.

Don'ts

Don't demand or confront.

✗

Don't bottle things up.

✗

Don't negate the differences
between men and women.

✗

Don't forget to be intimate
yourself – set an example.

PAST
relationships

Unless you are a complete novice at the love game then you will have had lovers in the past. So how much of this should you share with your current partner? Again it all depends on the couple but there are a few etiquette guidelines that always apply. For instance, calling out a past lover's name just as you climax with your current lover is definitely inexcusable. It is simply bad manners and must not be done. The same goes for calling your lover by the wrong name.

Don't show mementos or photos of your ex to your current partner. Wipe the slate clean with each new relationship.

KEEPING OLD PHOTOS

You can discuss past lovers if your current one wants to hear about them. If they don't, then don't. If you want to discuss what you and an old flame did in bed it is entirely up to your current partner if this is permissible. But asking for certain sex acts because your ex did them is not permissible. If you took erotic photos of your past lover then destroy them once the relationship is over. Keeping them and showing them to your new partner is definitely wrong – the same goes for movies, videos, and even love letters. Come to each new relationship afresh.

And not only shouldn't you call your present lover by a previous lover's name but you also shouldn't refer to any parts of your, or her, body by pet names you may have enjoyed in the past. Don't keep personal mementos of a sexual nature or go all wistful when a particular piece of music is played if it was special in a previous relationship.

STARTING AFRESH

In an ideal world your sex life with your current partner should start completely afresh – buy new bedding, change the décor in the bedroom, and indulge in new sexual pursuits. Unfortunately we don't live in an ideal world so you will have to make the most of what you've got – but do it with good manners and bear in mind that your partner wants to feel like they are your very first lover even if they aren't.

At the beginning of a new relationship you have to assume that it is going to last and that means getting it off to a good start by attempting to purge the evidence of all old relationships. Put the photos of your past lover away, change the sheets, and behave as if this is the first time for both of you. You'll make your new partner feel comfortable and have a better chance of success, and your relationship lasting, if you do so.

Dos

Do find out how much about your past sex life
your current partner wants to
know – and stick to it.

✓

Do throw away any photos, videos,
and letters that relate to past relationships.

Don'ts

Don't call a new lover by an
old lover's name – ever.

✗

Don't keep mementos of old flames.

sexually and romantically

Sex and romance are obviously linked, and mutually dependent and necessary, you can't have one without the other. Or if you could would you want to? It is said that women seek romance and men want sex. This may or may not be true or may in reality depend on the individuals. What is possibly true is that one part of a couple – be it the man or the woman – will at times want more sex than romance and during others more romance than sex, and again at other times equal shares of both. Or maybe sometimes one partner doesn't want either sex or romance. What is also true is that you have to give as much as you want to receive.

Being nice to each other shouldn't be an effort. Breakfast in bed is always a treat.

BEING AT EASE WITH OURSELVES

If you are in a relationship because you need to prop up a flagging ego or need to improve your self-esteem then you will look to your partner to provide all the support you cannot give yourself. This can be extremely dangerous to the relationship. If, on the other hand, you are already at ease with yourself then you don't need a partner to prop you up. You are then free to provide any support that they might need. A relationship of two emotionally strong people works best – it is much harder if one of the couple is defective in some way and seeks too much support from the other.

ENJOYING EACH OTHER

If you want a great time in the bedroom then your seduction, foreplay, and passion must begin outside of it. If you want your romance and intimacy to be heightened then perhaps you need to begin in the bedroom. A couple who make love frequently and enjoyably will be much closer than one that doesn't. A couple who spend a lot of time non-sexually touching will enjoy pleasuring each other more. Making your partner breakfast in bed isn't a chore but foreplay in a sense. Giving your partner a loving and soothing massage is intimate and doesn't have to be sexual – but the sex later (even if that is days later) will be more rewarding and enjoyable because of it.

BEING FRIENDS

You need, as a couple, to be not only lovers but also friends – and best friends at that. And you have to treat each other with the respect that friends give each other.

Some couples seem to be at each other's throats all the time; arguing;

A relationship shouldn't be about emotional dependency, it should be fun – enjoy yourselves!

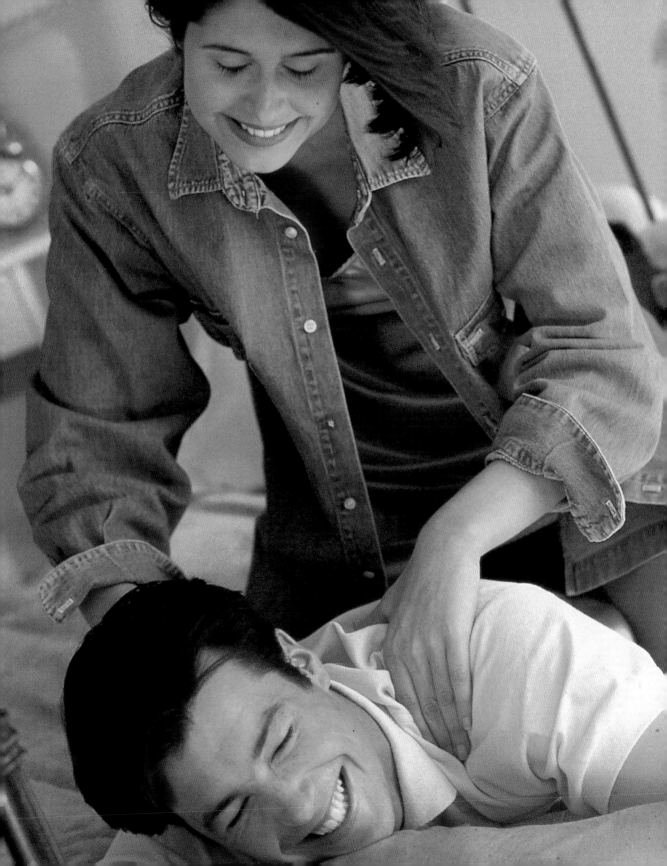

quarrelling; being distant from each other, verbally abusive, and even violent – that's no way to behave with someone you want to be intimate with, have sex with, and make love with.

You not only have to respect your partner as an individual but must also respect their sex in general. If you are a man you have to like women to be really able to relate to your partner; if you are a woman you have to like men to be really able to relate to your partner – and this is where the real trouble often lies. You may have been drawn to your partner in the first place because they are an exception, someone who doesn't conform to the standard for their gender, and you are attracted to that. However, you will have to learn to accept the things that they have in common with their sex that you will undoubtedly find. Learn to appreciate the differences between you as well as taking on board interests you share with them.

Being romantically and sexually nice to each other isn't difficult – it's something we all seem to do a lot of when we first meet someone but it can fade away as the years go on. You have to reintroduce an element of courtship, of grace and politeness, and of seduction and charm to keep your passion alive.

Be romantic, be surprising, be the first.

BEING NICE TO EACH OTHER

It's more romantic to slip a note under your loved one's pillow to say "I love you" than to nag them about how bad they look first thing in the morning. Being the first to offer to bring breakfast in bed isn't giving in or thinking the other lazy – it's being nice. You don't have to wait for festive seasons or birthdays to give surprise presents – give them every day, they don't have to cost anything, just be a surprise. Write your partner a love letter; remind them of how you first made love; bring them flowers; run them a bath; hold hands; unexpectedly kiss the back of their neck and tell them they smell good; compliment them on their ideas, creative talents, original inventive thoughts; flatter them; praise them; ask their advice; and listen to them (make sure you do that one a lot). Look into your partner's eyes when you make love; take time and trouble over them; remember why you are together; tell them you love them at every possible opportunity; plan the future together; spend leisure time together and cultivate things you do together. You must go out of your way to make their life enjoyable, exciting, different, and stimulating – if you are a delight to be around then you will both benefit from it enormously. The more you have in common the more you'll have.

DOS

Do be nice to each other.

✓

Do find time to be intimate and romantic.

✓

Do appreciate the differences.

✓

Do be gentle with each other.

✓

Do treat each other like friends as well as lovers.

DON'TS

Don't wait to be romantic – surprise them.

✗

Don't take each other for granted.

✗

Don't bore each other.

✗

Don't ever assume anything.

PART TWO

MAINLY
for men

When most men first meet their partners they usually put on a bit of a show, dress smartly, are polite and attentive, and make love with infinite patience and care. A few years down the line things tend to be allowed to slip a bit. Perhaps you no longer shave every day, (especially on weekends) you dress in your shabbiest casual clothes, and you forget the tenderness you once showed to your lover. This section is about going back to those early days and rediscovering the techniques of courting, politeness, and seduction. After all, if you are not seducing your lover each and every time you make love, then what are you doing?

Do you know what your partner prefers you to wear in bed and how they like you to undress? And are you responsible for the tears and rough patches in your relationship? Do you know how to bring your partner to a deeper and greater sexual satisfaction? Men and women do have different approaches to both sex and intimacy but this section should help you understand what your partner wants and ensure that you are both working toward the same thing – greater fulfillment in your relationship.

You need to be supportive of your partner and aware of her needs and desires.

Different perspectives

All men approach bedroom manners with a different perspective – and this will obviously also depend on what their partner tolerates and needs. However, there are a few guidelines that apply to all men in a relationship; how to give and receive oral sex, the art of lovemaking, and personal hygiene for example. You also need to be supportive of your partner when she doesn't want sex and need to know how to ask for sex without demanding it (or sulking if you don't get it).

Men have differing approaches to making love, but certain rules apply to all men.

THE ART OF GIVING
oral sex

There are no real rules but there is some etiquette involved if you are performing oral sex on your partner. The most important lesson is don't do it if she doesn't want you to. You must discuss it first, rather than trying to pressure her.

KEEP ALERT

When you are giving your partner oral sex you must make sure you concentrate on her pleasure. After all, it is her that you are doing it for. Make sure you listen to her preferences; vary the way that you suck and lick the clitoris and anything else – be responsive to your partner's needs. You can use your finger to pull upward on her pubic bone to allow better access to the clitoris.

You should also make sure that you do not neglect the rest of her body while you are giving oral sex. Try caressing her all over at the same time – this will give her heightened pleasure.

Be careful about your techniques. Blowing into the vagina is dangerous and should never be done. And make sure that you don't use your teeth. Cunnilingus needs only your tongue and lips, and perhaps your fingers, in this sensitive area so don't bite. Also try to keep your teeth from touching the clitoris.

LET HER TAKE CONTROL

There may be times when your partner needs more pressure or speed than you can give her, so do not be offended if she takes over and masturbates herself with her fingers or a vibrator. After she has come she may want you to stop touching her

immediately as the whole area may become too sensitive, so she may push your hand or head away – don't be offended by this. And always give her time to recover before attending to your own needs if you haven't already come. That is good manners.

COMMENTING DURING ORAL SEX

You should ensure that you don't make any personal comments about your partner's body unless they are positive. Some women become very moist as they come (or even before). This isn't dangerous moisture and you can taste it without risk to health or hygiene, but perhaps your partner might not want you to make a joke of it or pass any comment at all. However, some women find it quite a turn-on to be told how sweet they taste during and after oral sex.

Let your partner set the pace when it comes to oral sex.

Dos

Do vary the way you suck and lick the clitoris.

✓

Do use your fingers to gain
better access to her clitoris.

✓

Do allow her time to recover before attending
to your needs (assuming you haven't come first).

Don'ts

Don't use your teeth at all.

✗

Don't blow into the vagina.

✗

Don't be offended if she takes over.

✗

Don't make personal comments
unless they are positive ones.

✗

Don't get so into it that you forget
to caress the rest of her body.

THE ART OF RECEIVING
oral sex

Receiving oral pleasure from your partner is a favor not a right – don't demand it.

Having your partner perform oral sex on you isn't a right, it's an honor and a privilege. Obviously, if you want your lover to perform oral sex on you as part of your normal lovemaking then you must observe a few rules of good manners or you will turn them off completely. For instance, if you thrust too hard she will choke, and that may well make her reticent to try again – so be considerate.

You must give her room to breathe otherwise it will be an extremely unpleasant experience for her. And the most important thing to remember is that your partner is getting very intimate with your genitals so you must make sure your hygiene is up to scratch before asking her to perform oral sex on you.

BE A MAN ABOUT IT

You must be aware that your partner will sometimes not want to give you oral sex, but on other occasions may be very willing. Accept whatever her decision is with grace, and possibly suggest some other activity that you can both enjoy together if she does not want to. It is also true that some women find the taste of semen unpleasant, so even if your partner is willing, she may not want you to ejaculate in her mouth. Offer her an alternative before she has to say anything as that could make her uncomfortable. An idea is for her to give you oral sex until you almost climax and then you could come over her breasts or into a kleenex. Or make a game of it and see how far you can come.

THINK ABOUT YOUR PARTNER

You must be responsible even during oral sex. If you know that one of you has a sexually transmitted disease, NEVER let your partner give you oral sex without putting a condom on first. You may not want to in the heat of the moment but you really don't have a choice.

Oral sex is an intimate act that you should enjoy alongside your partner, rather than just letting her pleasure you. She may like you to talk to her while she is doing it but don't be coarse – she is being loving and will not want that in return. And make sure you don't get so wrapped up in the pleasure that you forget that she may need to take a break. It is important not to be selfish because that could ruin the experience for both of you. Be careful about how you refer to oral sex: The terms "blow job" or "giving head" may be fine in the locker room but not in the bedroom. If you want to ask your partner for oral sex, why not say "pleasure me with your mouth"? It sounds better and more romantic.

DOS

Do treat it like a privilege
– not a right to be demanded.

✓

Do realize that your lover will sometimes
want to, and sometimes not want to.

✓

Do allow her the choice of whether
you ejaculate in her mouth, or wherever else.

✓

Do allow your lover to take
a break if she needs to.

DON'TS

Don't forget your personal hygiene for such an
intensely intimate act.

✗

Don't be coarse when referring to oral sex.

✗

Don't hold her head to your
groin – give her room to breathe.

✗

Don't have oral sex without a condom unless
you are sure you are both free from any sexually
transmitted diseases – and that includes AIDS.

✗

Don't thrust so hard you gag her.

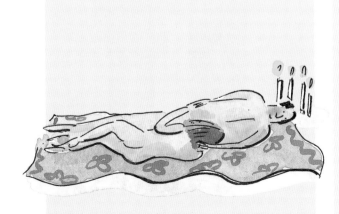

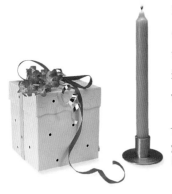

HOW TO ASK FOR SEX
without demanding

It is generally accepted that men are quicker to get ready for sex, and quicker to satisfy, than women. Women generally need a longer warm-up time and more time spent on foreplay, seduction, romancing, and intimacy. If you go at it like a bull in a china shop you'll only end up with broken crockery. It's your job to respect your partner's need for these things and to provide them for her. You have to look at your approach if there's a problem with your sex life.

Take time to romance your partner and create intimacy for good sex.

You must be considerate of your partner's sexual needs and allow her time to get ready, time to warm up, and time to enjoy sex. You should see yourself as the choreographer. You have to put in considerable time and effort beforehand and not just expect your lover to be ready to make love at the drop of a hat. If your sex life is unsatisfactory you really only have yourself to blame. Put in the effort beforehand and your partner will want to be a full participant.

BEING CARED ABOUT AND VALUED
If you don't touch your partner romantically and charmingly during the day then don't expect her to be ready for love play at the end of the day. Women need to feel safe to make love – and that means feeling loved, respected, wanted, cared about, and valued. Your partner doesn't want to be seen as a sex object, she needs to be important to you as a lover and a friend as well as a sexual partner.

If you demand sex at any time you will kill any feelings of trust and love. If you threaten, sulk, or

Be together romantically before you expect to be together sexually.

If your sex life is unsatisfactory, then you only have yourself to blame.

display anger you are behaving badly. If you woo and court, romance and seduce, and show warmth and affection then you will get much more of a response. It is important to have good manners when it comes to having sex, after all you are inviting another human being to share her most inner and personal body parts with you in an act of intense and vulnerable intimacy. You have to approach your partner with an air of decorum, delicacy, tact, and courtesy. This isn't manipulation, merely good manners and respect.

Your partner is sensitive and emotional and needs to be approached with confidence and love rather than belligerence and demands. If you want your partner to indulge in any aspect of sex with you then you have to suggest and invite rather than order and demand.

Having sex with your lover isn't just a question of pressing the right buttons to get the responses you want. It's about making sure she is sexually and emotionally satisfied. You need to spend time understanding what it is that your partner likes and dislikes, needs and wants. You have to spend time getting her juices flowing – and that means you have to become a sexual expert. You have to know your way around your woman's body, understand her sexuality, discover her preferences and desires, take on board her quirks, and co-operate in her fantasies. By doing this you will get all the sex you want – and a truly happy and sexually satisfied partner – without any demanding.

HOW TO TALK FLUENT WOMAN

Most importantly you have to spend time outside of the bedroom being a considerate lover to get really good results. You need to be a friend, confidante, conversationalist, humorist, and preferably a good cook. In short you need to be bilingual, and know how to talk fluent woman. You need to understand how your lover thinks and feels before you can expect to know how she makes love. If you haven't cooked her a fine meal with good wine and all the trimmings do you really expect her to fall into your bed and be passionate? If you haven't listened to her troubles, treated her fairly and equally, and been kind do you really expect her to bestow ecstasy on you?

Women are sensitive creatures who want romance and emotional support as well as physical satisfaction.

Dos

Do understand and know your
partner's sexual needs.

✓

Do allow her lots of time to get ready for sex.

✓

Do practice seduction and romance.

✓

Do be a kind, confident, and gentle lover.

Don'ts

Don't demand or assume anything.

✗

Don't rush your partner or force her
to do anything she doesn't want to.

✗

Don't sulk if she doesn't want to have
sex sometimes – be mature about it.

WHAT EVERY
man should wear in bed

All women are different and get turned on – and off – by different things but there are a few guidelines about what you should and shouldn't wear in bed. Obviously if you live alone and feel the cold, then wear whatever you want. But when you are going to bed with a

Pajamas may be cozy and warm in winter – but does your partner find them sexy?

partner you should bear in mind that she may not find this look very sexy. Silk boxer shorts are a good choice.

INVEST IN THE BEST

Firstly, most women find the sight of a man dressed only in his underpants, shoes, and socks laughable rather than sexy – and laughable means they are laughing at you, not merely finding it a bit funny. Always take your shoes and socks off before taking your pants off.

Change your underpants and socks daily – it is no use wearing the right thing if it isn't clean. In hot weather it is often best to abandon socks altogether. And wearing no underwear under trousers, especially light cotton summer trousers, is also very sexy.

While you might find underwear with jokes or cartoons very amusing they simply aren't sexy to most women. The same goes for gray y-fronts, torn underwear, underwear that is too baggy or too small, and cheap and tacky underwear. Basically invest in the very best – and then wear it.

KEEP A LITTLE HIDDEN

Warm wooly dressing gowns are usually a turn-off. Silk smoking jackets can be very sexy if worn with style – they can be worn in bed and left for your lover to remove. Complete male nakedness in bed can be a bit daunting for your partner if everything is on display. It is better to leave a little to the imagination and something to be removed. Keeping your underwear on is fine – keeping your socks on isn't. Sweatshirts and T-shirts are fine if you're cold – undershirts aren't. Always wear underwear if you're wearing a T-shirt since the sight of male genitals poking out from under a T-shirt is faintly ridiculous, as is a spare tire bulging out anywhere. Slim is sexy; chubby isn't.

Even men should dress, and undress, to please.

Make sure that your underwear isn't your old wear. And no "jokey" boxers please!

COMPLETELY DRESSED

A lot of women do not find entire nudity as sexy as partial nudity so you should be aware of what your partner prefers. But what to keep on? Your socks? NO! Try wearing a silk bathrobe or a pair of very tight-fitting trousers, with no underwear of course, or a pair of cotton boxer shorts. Going to bed dressed completely may be very sexy as well – especially if your partner is, on the other hand, completely naked. You can make love to her wearing your very best clothes and she will enjoy the caress of the materials against her skin.

TALK TO HER

Always remember that the secret of a good relationship is communication so talk to your lover, find out exactly what she finds sexy and unsexy, discuss what turns her on and off, and pay attention to her needs. Be aware of what it is she is saying and remember it – you will be amply rewarded.

So to recap, don't wear your oldest baggy clothes to make love – you may have an old "comfort" T-shirt, but wearing it before lovemaking won't set your partner on

Make love to her wearing your best clothes. She will love the sensation of the clothes against her skin.

fire. Wear sexy boxer shorts and a tight-fitting, clean T-shirt. Make sure you change your underwear every day and especially before making love. Bear in mind that although it might be cold, wearing your socks in bed simply isn't done – bad manners indeed.

Remember what you wore on your first date – and wear the same sort of thing. I bet you dressed up then to impress, to seduce, to win her over. Don't get sloppy once you are in a relationship – maintain the same high standards and then your sex life will really zing. Remember the old adage that you can never be too wealthy or too thin – and then lose that spare tire around the midriff. Nothing is more off-putting to a woman than a man who has let himself go to seed.

DOS

Do take off your shoes and socks
before your trousers – always.

✓

Do change your underwear and socks daily.

✓

Do invest in the very best underwear
– and that means silk or pure cotton;
nylon isn't sexy at all, ever.

✓

Do wear a T-shirt rather than an undershirt.
Do wear your underwear if you keep
a T-shirt on.

✓

Do find out what your partner prefers you to
wear in bed and buy it.

DON'TS

Don't wear old or shabby underwear.

✗

Don't wear your socks in bed.

✗

Don't wear anything you wouldn't want to be
seen in on a first date – keep your standards up.

✗

Don't wear a spare tire around your midriff –
losing weight is the best attire you could present
to any woman.

YOUR
masturbation

Research has indicated that most men, even in a stable and loving relationship, will still masturbate alone from time to time. This is natural and has very little to do with sex; it is more a stress relieving technique or possibly stems from habit. Private male masturbation should be exactly that – private. Mutual masturbation on the other hand is by its very nature done together. This is a very different thing. If you've never tried it then do so, as it's an important part of lovemaking.

PRIVATE

There are some things that should be kept to yourself.

When you masturbate in private you may use erotic images to aid you; when you masturbate in front of your partner you will have her there as a stimulation. The two different types of masturbation shouldn't get confused or their boundaries become blurred. What you do in private is entirely your own business but when you are with your lover there is a whole new set of etiquette guidelines.

TAKE YOUR TIME
When you masturbate with your partner, your orgasm may be important but you must realize that so is your partner's pleasure. If you masturbate quickly to orgasm she may not enjoy watching you as much as if you take your time and put on a show for her. On the other hand, if she masturbates in front of you, she will need to achieve orgasm (that's the whole point) but you can also encourage, help if she wants you to, and be appreciative. Allow her to feel relaxed enough to masturbate.

Mutual masturbation, in which you bring each other to orgasm, is an invaluable technique. It can be helpful if either of you doesn't feel like full sex because you are tired or unwell, or if your lover is recovering from childbirth or is heavily pregnant. This too has its own etiquette. For a start who should come first? Or do you try to come at the same time? If you do try to come at the same time you may well be concentrating on giving too much rather than receiving. It may be best to concentrate on each other's pleasure first – take turns, but make sure that it isn't only ever the same person who achieves orgasm first. Then there is the etiquette of who cleans up the wetness (*see pages 80–83*), what you do after you have come, and what you do after your partner has come. If it's your turn to come first then make sure you stay fully awake and energetic for your lover's orgasm.

Remember that your partner's pleasure is just as important as your own.

BE IMAGINATIVE

There is nothing worse than when a woman gives her partner an orgasm only to have him virtually fall asleep while stimulating her. Be interested, co-operative, imaginative, and confident. Do what she likes best and do it well otherwise there's no point in doing it at all. And make sure she does what you like best – tell her what you like and how you like it. You are both entitled to the very best orgasm possible and, if you are reticent about voicing your own needs and wants, you could go through an entire relationship sexually unhappy and unsatisfied. And you wouldn't want that.

If your lover is the one to come first make sure she has time to get her breath back before pleasuring you. You could even forgo your orgasm occasionally if she needs to sleep immediately after coming. Whatever she wants is fine.

APPRECIATING IT

Be appreciative about receiving masturbation from your partner. Tell her when it is good. Praise her abilities. And don't concentrate so exclusively on your own orgasm that you forget she is there; you are allowed to kiss her when you come, look into her eyes, hold her, keep caressing her, cuddle up to her afterward – be loving at all times and you will both enjoy it far more.

Masturbating in front of each other or doing it to each other requires trust and security. It is a very personal and intimate act and you both need to feel safe and loved. You have to create the right atmosphere so that your partner will not feel intimidated or confronted. Male sexuality is lusty and can be sexually aggressive. You have to learn to be gentle and considerate. The language you use will demonstrate this to her. Use the term "masturbation" rather than any of the cruder, coarser terms there are for this act. And when you request her to masturbate you, make sure you are asking and not demanding – it's an honor she bestows, not a right.

Make sure you stay awake if she needs you to. Falling asleep straight after lovemaking is plain selfish!

Dos

Do be considerate with your ejaculate.

✓

Do it as much for your partner as for yourself.

✓

Do be gentle and considerate.

Don'ts

Don't be too quick or too selfish.

✗

Don't fall asleep immediately after coming.

✗

Don't always be the first, or last, to come.

ALL ABOUT
orgasms

Men and woman both have orgasms – they're different, that's all. Yours is more eruptive and messy; your partner's are probably multiple and more internal. There may be other differences such as depth, intensity, recovery rate,

We all have different tastes. Be sensitive to your partner's likes and dislikes.

and frequency but you should be the one to take charge of the mess that you will most certainly make. Make sure you take responsibility for your own semen.

USING FORETHOUGHT

If the climax takes place while you are inside your partner then the mess may not be as noticeable but it is there nevertheless. It is good manners to offer to get some kleenexes afterward – or whatever your partner prefers to use to clean herself with. Don't expect her to have to walk to the bathroom – go for her. If you have an orgasm externally there is a whole set of things to think of. For instance, semen stains clothing so if your lover is wearing her best silk dress she may not appreciate you climaxing over it. Likewise, semen in her hair may be acceptable to her (always ask first) if she is about to have a bath, but not if she's about to go out, so use a little forethought.

HAVE A PLAN

The male orgasm can be explosive at times and the direction, aim, and trajectory all need to be thought about. You may not have time if you are about to climax so think about it beforehand and have some sort of plan. This could be a simple as putting your hand in the way if your lover is masturbating you or turning to one side as you come, or even having some kleenexes ready.

The important rule to remember is that it is your semen, even after it has left your body, so you must take responsibility for it at all times. Be considerate about how you clean up afterward, be discreet if that is required, be respectful of your partner's preferences, and above all be responsible.

Some women have an aversion to semen while others find it tasty, healthy, and fun – only you will know which of these your partner is. It is likely that she will feel differently toward it at different times, so you must match your orgasms to her mood; use your judgment and common sense to avoid getting it wrong.

GOOD TIMING

Another important aspect of your orgasm is timing. Do you come before or after your partner, or at the same time? What does she prefer? What happens after you have come? You should vary who comes first so that you can both have the opportunity to fall asleep in a postorgasmic afterglow. If your lover comes first then give her time to get her breath back before she pleasures you. Allow her a break.

Be discreet, considerate, and responsible so you can enjoy that postorgasmic afterglow.

Remember that it is not a matter of life or death if you don't have an orgasm; occasionally bring your partner to orgasm and then let her go to sleep without having to reciprocate – she'll be flattered and honored.

LIKE CHOCOLATE

Make sure your partner has enough orgasms. Orgasms are like chocolates for women, one is never enough. This doesn't mean she always has to have more than one (or even one at all if she doesn't feel like it), but be prepared to offer more, and mean it when you do.

Make sure you know exactly what sort of orgasms your partner likes – and yes, there is more than one sort – and that you vary the tempo, pressure, tension, and urgency of your fingers, tongue, or penis action so that she remains excited and never gets bored. Boring your partner during sex is unforgivable.

To be really good at sex you have to study and learn. For instance, there are three types of orgasm – clitoral, vaginal, and G-spot – do you know how your partner responds to each? Can you use more than one type at a time? Varying what you do sustains an interest and enthusiasm. If you always do what you've always done, you'll always get the same responses – don't you want some variety? If you are in any doubt try asking her what she likes.

Good sex is rewarding and relaxing – make time for it. Hurried lovemaking will leave you both unsatisfied.

Dos

Do take responsibility for your semen at all times.

✓

Do have a plan as to what you are going to do with it.

✓

Do vary who comes first.

✓

Do clean up after yourself in all circumstances.

Don'ts

Don't expect your partner always to be as delighted to see your semen as you are.

✗

Don't forget it's a personal and intimate act so use your discretion.

✗

Don't delay cleaning up – do it at once.

PERSONAL
hygiene

If you are inviting someone into your bed then you have a duty and responsibility to make sure that your personal hygiene is of the very highest standard. After all, you are inviting someone to share a very personal and intimate space. You may be planning sex, or alternatively just sleeping, but it is still important to get your hygiene right.

Good personal hygiene is important. Lousy hygiene makes for an inconsiderate lover.

NOT JUST A QUICK WASH

If you are going to make love you should always shower and brush your teeth, but is there even more you can do? What about breath freshening? You should also make sure that your nails – both fingers and toes – are clean, cut, and filed; that you use a suitable deodorant; and that your hair is clean and well groomed. It may be nice first thing in the morning, before you kiss your lover, if you brush your teeth and use a breath freshener. If you need to shave frequently (twice a day) make sure you do so before making love because stubble burn is painful and uncomfortable.

FINDING THE RIGHT
PLACE TO DEAL WITH PIMPLES

We all get pimples from time to time – the etiquette of these irritating skin blemishes is to keep them to yourself. Don't pick them or interfere with them in any way in public – and that means even in the sanctity of your own bedroom; your lover deserves more respect than

that. Similarly don't scratch, fidget, blow your nose, pass gas, burp, or pick wax out of your ears in bed – go to the bathroom and do these things (that we do all have to do) in private; try to retain a little mystery and a little decorum. Be discreet about bodily functions.

"Stubble burn" is painful – always shave first. Your lover will appreciate your thoughtfulness.

Make sure your oral hygiene is maintained – give your partner a fresh morning kiss.

SHARING YOUR BOUDOIR

When you get undressed for bed (*see page 64*) fold your clothes up neatly rather than dropping them on the floor in a heap – unless of course you are having sudden and raunchy sex. Even in the latter case, you should put the things away afterward. Your partner won't want to see a pile of messy clothes – they are your responsibility so put them away. Watch what you eat and drink before making love – no one likes strong garlic fumes or beery breath when they are kissing.

The etiquette of bedroom manners is to be aware that you are sharing the space with your lover. Try to remain conscious that what you say with your body speaks volumes about yourself and how much respect you have for her. If you get out of bed, yawn, scratch your groin, pass gas, and sniff you'll be presenting an image of someone who doesn't really care. If, on the other hand, you get out of bed with grace and dignity and brush your teeth before kissing her you'll be saying how much she means to you – good manners indeed.

If, by accident, you have to pass gas in bed try to do it in a dignified manner. Apologize and don't make a big thing of it. Don't bury your head under the sheets, breathe in deep, and shout "wow!" That's simply bad manners.

KEEP IT GLAMOROUS

Keep the bedroom for its original purpose – going to bed. Don't store old motorbike engines in there or use it as a part-time office. Keep it glamorous and sexy, well decorated and luxurious. When your partner wants to make love she will be more relaxed and feel safe if the room is conducive to sex and love rather than if it looks like a factory storage room. Use the most luxurious fabrics; lots of candles (candlelight is so sexy); lots of cushions; sexy music; food and wine; and make sure you have a handy drawer for sex toys, condoms, and kleenexes. But, most importantly, keep your personal hygiene to the very highest standard imaginable if you want to maintain a pleasing and satisfying sex life.

Be considerate of your partner's space and tidy up neatly after yourself.

Dos

Do remember what the bedroom is for.

✓

Do treat the bedroom
(and your lover) with respect.

✓

Do keep the bedroom tidy.

✓

Do maintain high standards of personal hygiene.

✓

Do watch your diet before making
love – not too much garlic, red wine,
or spicy food.

Don'ts

Don't scratch, burp, pass gas,
or pick pimples in front of your lover.

✗

Don't make love without first
bathing, shaving, and brushing your teeth.

✗

Don't wear anything old, worn, crumpled,
or creased if you are going to make love.

✗

Don't assume your lover finds anything
acceptable (or unacceptable) – check first
and continue to ask her regularly because she
may change her mind.

CONDOMS, WET PATCHES,
and other things

There is a whole range of bedroom equipment that can give rise to problems if not discussed. Obviously within the boundaries of a warm and loving relationship every aspect of lovemaking will be discussed and jointly agreed upon, but there are some areas that the man really should take the responsibility for. But don't ever assume, always discuss first.

Use a condom if required to do so. Ask your partner to choose her favorite kind.

It was said earlier that you should go and get kleenexes for your woman, but it should really be your job to make sure they are always provided and that they are easy to reach, while at the same time in a discreet place. And make sure the kleenexes are suitable, romantic, and tasteful; your partner will not want you to throw over a roll of toilet paper – offer her a delicate box of rose-tinted kleenexes instead. And NEVER wipe semen off with an old T-shirt or your socks.

A MAN'S GOTTA DO
WHAT A MAN'S GOTTA DO

If you wear condoms then it's your job to provide them, to make sure they are within their sell-by date, and to ensure they fit properly. You should also be responsible for the disposing of them afterward in a safe and hygienic way. And, of course, you should offer your partner a choice; she may like ribbed ones, or flavored ones, or even glow-in-the-dark ones, you never know. Even if you know your partner takes a contraceptive pill you should still ask if she wants you to use a condom – after all she may have forgotten to take the pill or may have run out.

There is also the question of who puts the condom on. Some men like to do it themselves while some women enjoy helping – you decide between you and make sure the moment when you need it is not clumsy and embarrassing – be open and honest about your preferences.

AND ANOTHER THING...

So who sleeps in the wet patch? Well, it depends on whose wet patch it is. If it is caused by you then it is obviously your responsibility; if it is caused by your partner being moist during orgasm then technically it's hers, but as a gentleman you would still offer, wouldn't you? Being the first to take responsibility is a good thing. It's a better lover who isn't lazy about these things. Make sure it's you who remembers to change the sheets (and you who washes them of course), provides the candles, and checks the condoms. Being the first to do this is a sign of respect, interest, and concern – all good things.

Talk to your partner about what you want and who is responsible for what in the relationship.

CHARGING THE BATTERIES

Couples often introduce an element of sex aids and toys into their love play at some stage in their relationship. Make sure you discuss the possibility with your partner before buying her a vibrator for instance. And all these aids again have their own etiquette. For instance, the batteries of vibrators need to be changed from time to time as there is nothing worse than a flat battery just when you need power the most. Sex toys also need to be scrupulously cleaned after use – and that means immediately after use. They also need to be put away safely and discreetly. There is nothing worse than the cleaner finding your vibrator – unless of course it's your mother who finds it!

WHY TURNING ON CAN BE A TURN OFF

If you use erotic literature or images as part of your love play then you have a duty to make sure they aren't readily accessible to your children. Make sure you have a locked drawer to keep them in – under the mattress

Dressing to please can be fun – keep special clothes ready to change into quickly, just in case.

isn't a safe place. It is the first place children look. The same goes for videos and movies. And if you do want to watch erotic videos then make sure your partner is of the same mind first. There is no greater turn off than someone watching some sex act on video and getting turned on while you are bored and turned off. Only involve videos if your partner really wants to as well. Wait and see if she suggests watching one.

KEEPING CLOTHES SPECIAL

You and your partner might like to wear special outfits for romantic evenings. Keep these outfits just for that. Even if you don't care about clothing, your partner may. If she has a favorite pair of ripped jeans or an old leather jacket she likes you to wear when making love then keep them special. She will be offended if she finds you working in the backyard in them. They are special to her, so keep them special for you too.

Sex toys are fun, but it is vital to keep vibrators clean between uses.

Sexy videos are a matter of personal taste. Only watch them if you both want to.

Dos

Do provide good quality kleenexes.

✓

Do take responsibility for any mess you make.

✓

Do be gallant when it comes to wet patches.

✓

Do make sure any sex aids or toys are
kept clean and are put away safely and securely.

Don'ts

Don't forget other people's sensitivities,
particularly if you have children, when it comes
to your own sexuality.

✗

Don't ever run out of condoms.

✗

Don't buy vibrators or sexy lingerie for your
lover without first checking their suitability –
your taste isn't necessarily theirs.

THE ART OF
lovemaking

When you approach your lover to make love, you have to be aware that her mood, physical requirements, emotional needs, mental outlook, desires, needs, and wants all change from day to day – as do yours. You, however, know how you feel and what you want. But what about your partner? How do you know what she needs and wants? How are you going to approach her if you don't know? If you are in constant physical and emotional touch with her during the day, then you will have a much better idea of her needs than if you are blunt, too quick, or too assuming in your approach. Intimacy leads to sex; closeness is a forerunner of foreplay. You have to be romantically close to be in touch – that's good etiquette as well as good sense.

Consider your partner's feelings as a whole: her mood, emotions, desires, and physical needs.

SPIRITUAL AS WELL AS SEXUAL

If you approach your partner from a place of love and trust you will find that your lovemaking takes on a deeper dimension of enhanced spirituality as well as physicality. Once in the bedroom and ready to make love you should maintain the highest standards of respect. This may mean that you sometimes delay your orgasm until she is fully satisfied. Make sure you are a considerate, confident, and experienced lover – give her time to enjoy sex; think of her needs as much, if not more, than your own; be gentle, kind, and loving; be imaginative, creative, and stimulating in the bedroom; and, most importantly, engender an atmosphere of trust and respect.

If your partner isn't in the mood for sex then accept it and don't sulk or be belligerent. If, on the other hand, she is in the mood for raunchy, explicit sex then go along with it and enjoy it. But if your partner needs gentle lovemaking be considerate and moderate. You might think that all this is letting your partner set the tone and mood for love making – it is. If you let your partner decide and choose then in return she will be willing, co-operative, imaginative, spontaneous, and energetic because she will feel relaxed and secure with you. Sex is the closest we will ever get to another human being as an adult and it should be treated with a certain reverence and respect. This doesn't mean it can't be fun as well – just be aware of how intimate it is and treat your partner respectfully and allow trust to develop between you.

The act of making love can be pleasurable and spiritual all at the same time.

There's no need to rush your lovemaking sessions.
Always take a break for a little light refreshment.

GIVING YOUR PARTNER SPACE

If you partner is pregnant or recovering from
childbirth then forgo full penetrative sex (or let her
decide how much she can cope with) and suggest
mutual masturbation instead. Don't pressure your
partner into sex when she can't cope with it
physically. The same goes generally if she is tired,
unwell, or upset. Give her the space to feel relaxed
and comfortable.

When you are making love make sure your
lover achieves orgasm as many times as she needs
or wants to. If, after orgasm, she doesn't want you
to touch her because she feels too sensitive then
give her time to recover. Provide a little food and
wine if she wants to have a break. And make sure
you always keep things from getting too serious –
laughter is good for both of you.

Don't expect your partner to make love if she
doesn't feel right about it. You might feel like sex
outdoors but if it's raining or too cold then she
may well reject your advances – don't take this
personally, accept that the weather conditions
aren't right even if you don't mind the cold or the
wet yourself.

TAKE YOUR TIME – IT'S NOT A RACE

Take your time when you make love and don't go
at it as if it is a race. It is an experience to be
savored, enjoyed, and relished – you can't do any of
this if you rush it. And don't, after you have come,
collapse onto your partner. You must take your
weight on your elbows – she won't want your full
weight on her.

Dos

Do choreograph the lovemaking
so your partner is fully satisfied.

✓

Do provide a warm and safe environment so she
will feel secure and relaxed for making love.

✓

Do be considerate and confident
in your lovemaking.

✓

Do be aware of the physical limitations
your partner may have and be
gentlemanly – take the weight.

Don'ts

Don't demand or sulk if she
doesn't want to make love.

✗

Don't be too quick – give her
the time to enjoy sex with you.

PART THREE

MAINLY

for women

ost women want their lovers to be supportive, caring, gentle, and respectful – as well as great in bed. As women's roles in bed have changed so dramatically over the past few decades, some men have got a little confused about what they are supposed to be doing and how they are supposed to behave. This section explores female sexuality and reveals how to enjoy and ask for pretty well anything you want without causing your partner to leave home in shock and horror.

What sort of man have you got?

You need to know how to get your lover to be intimate, warm, respectful, as well as wild and raunchy when the time is right. In order to do this, you need to know what sort of man you've got and be polite enough to allow him his own views and reactions. For example, what do you do about menstruation and personal hygiene? For some men this whole area is shrouded in mystery and they would prefer it to remain like that; others are open and understanding and you can change your tampon in front of them with impunity. Do you know what type of man yours is? This will have a bearing on the whole of your sex life so it is important that you find out.

Following the rules

You might think that there aren't any rules in the bedroom and essentially that is true, but there are still a few guidelines that you may wish to follow so you can enjoy all aspects of your sexuality with your partner to the fullest. There is, for instance, an etiquette for oral sex – how to give it and how to receive it. It is also important to know how to say no to sex without causing a sulk at the same time. And what to wear to look like a sex goddess.

Exploring your sexuality will unlock your potential.

What sort of man have you got? Are you sensitive to how he will react to certain sexual situations?

THE ART OF GIVING
oral sex

A little practice never hurt anyone. You can perfect your oral techniques using a Popsicle.

You might think that any man would be so glad of oral sex that he wouldn't consider how it is given – wrong. To maintain good etiquette there are a few rules to follow. Firstly, NEVER make comparisons. You might think that saying his is bigger or better than any others you've enjoyed orally would be good – wrong again. It sets up seeds of discontent.

Remember what you are there for – pleasing your partner orally. Don't glance at your watch, look bored, or watch television. Look up adoringly at him, listen to what he wants, and let him have it. If he needs firm pressure, fast action, and lots of moaning then be accommodating, be sexy, be a participant because you can, and should, enjoy this too. But be in control. Don't let him thrust so hard that you can't breathe. Keep one hand on his pubic area so you can push back if you need to. Use your other hand to stimulate him, caress his testicles, or masturbate him as you suck.

TELL HIM BEFOREHAND
It is always best to tell your partner if you really don't feel comfortable giving him oral sex. But do ask yourself first why you do not feel able to if he particularly enjoys it. If you really feel you can't, offer an exciting alternative when you tell him.

If you are giving oral sex, bring your partner to orgasm in the way that is best for you but let him think it's best for him. For instance, if you don't want him to come

in your mouth then it's polite to tell him – but don't say it's because his semen tastes horrid and you feel sick. Instead tell him you prefer to see him come over your breasts since it turns you on more. Tell him at the beginning and then he won't be disappointed. If you're not sure about how to give good oral sex you are allowed to practice; try a Popsicle or a large sausage. The best way would be to share the practice session and try it out on him.

Derogatory comments about your partner's size is the ultimate in insensitivity. Never make comparisons – they're all fabulous!

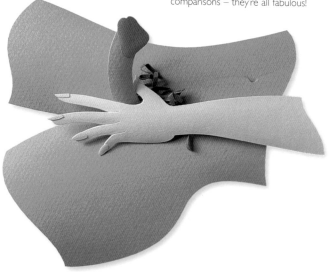

Dos

Do stay in control and
focus on what you are doing.

✓

Do try to please him by making
it as sexy as possible for him.

✓

Do vary what you are doing – from kissing
his penis to actual sucking and licking.

✓

Do be aware of when he is about to come
if you don't want him to come in your mouth.

Don'ts

Don't try and make him feel grateful because
you are doing him a favor. Treat him lovingly.

✗

Don't look at the clock or watch television.

✗

Don't do it if you don't want to.

✗

Don't blow down your partner's penis.

✗

Don't bite.

✗

Don't let him thrust too
hard – you set the agenda.

THE ART OF RECEIVING
oral sex

Take control and guide your partner during oral sex – tell him what you like and don't like.

Some women enjoy having their partner perform oral sex on them; some complain that their partners won't, and some women don't like it at all. It is such a personal thing that no advice can be given as to whether it should form part of your lovemaking or not – it is entirely up to you as a couple. The problems only occur when one of the couple wants to and the other doesn't – or the one doing it is inexperienced, clumsy, or lacks finesse.

HELPING YOUR PARTNER

You will need to spread your thighs wide so that your partner will be able to breathe while he is giving you oral sex. Try and remember to think of him at the same time as enjoying what he is doing! He will need to rest at times because giving cunnilingus can be exhausting to the tongue muscles.

Do let your partner know when you are reaching orgasm, as it is important for a man to get feedback. In fact you should let your partner know exactly what is going on for you at all times – if you are enjoying it, if they are hitting the right spot, if what they are doing is a bit painful or unexciting. You can do this with noises, movements, words, or any other method you can devise. The important thing is to let him know; it will make it easier for him next time, and much better for you. You should tell him how it is best for you to achieve orgasm. After all it is your orgasm, and the more you tell him the better it will be for you. Better still, show him.

It is especially important to communicate if your clitoral area becomes too sensitive, or if you know you won't be able to achieve an orgasm. Without this sort of information, your partner could feel like he has failed and not know why.

DON'T FAKE IT

Any sound, strong relationship is based on trust, respect, and good communication. If you fake it, you've blown it. Honesty is best. If you can't make it then just tell him. It is better to own up than to act out. That doesn't mean to say you can't act a little – throw in the odd moan, be vocal, writhe a little. You don't have to ham it up but you can please your partner by being active – a participant.

A HELPING HAND

There may be times when you need extra pressure, particularly if your partner is getting tired. You can either use your own fingers or a vibrator. As long as you have discussed this beforehand your man won't feel rejected. Let him know how you react when you're about to come as he may decide to take a break at just the wrong moment. If he knows to continue he will for your benefit.

DOS

Do let your partner breathe.

✓

Do let your partner rest.

✓

Do give your partner feedback.

✓

Do tell your partner if your
clitoral area becomes sensitive.

DON'TS

Don't be shy about telling your
partner what you want them to do.

✗

Don't fake it – don't ever fake anything.

✗

Don't worry if you want to help out
with your fingers or a vibrator.

HOW TO PLEASE YOUR LOVER
without becoming a sex slave

If you are in a full and rewarding relationship then sex will play an important part of that relationship. Your partner will have needs, desires, and activities that he likes to indulge in and enjoy. You will also have ideas of your own. Putting the two together is a fundamental part of having successful relationship. If one of you only wants tender lovemaking and the other always wants raunchy sex then you will have to learn to compromise and take turns. When one of you simply refuses to budge then you have serious problems. Remember, if you want, you must be prepared to give.

Romance and sex can be the same thing if you both learn to compromise.

COMMUNICATION AND COMPROMISE

You obviously have to have your partner's full co-operation in getting what you want as well as in helping him to find his own satisfaction. Key words here are communication and compromise. Firstly you have to know what your partner wants in the way of sex and he in turn must also know what you want. Perhaps he likes you to dress up and act out some fantasy for him. You in turn might like him to touch you lovingly during the day, hold hands, and be romantic. It isn't suggested that you use sex as a bargaining tool, merely that you enter into a spirit of mutual cooperation and then you will both end up happy with what you get.

No woman should be expected to be a sex slave. But if you are in a sexually active relationship with your partner then you must want him to be sexually satisfied and happy, and must know what it is he wants and be prepared to give it to him. If you are not then you need to ask yourself why not.

Perhaps their needs are too extreme or you feel them to be bizarre, unhygienic, or unhealthy. Then you must talk to your partner about toning them down or modifying them.

HOW TO FUEL YOUR LOVER'S FIRE

A lot of sexual relationships fail because one partner gets bored or feels that sex has lost its sparkle. You can help keep the flames of passion running high in your relationship, no matter how long you have been together, by being liberated and sexy. If you let sex become a routine or a chore then the whole relationship is in danger of falling apart. Only by communication can you know what fuels your lover's particular fire – and what made his heart race a year ago may not necessarily still have the same effect now.

Stay ahead of the game and monitor your partner's preferences.

Enter into sex as fully participating adults – discuss ways in which to spice up your sex life.

BEING ALL WOMEN TO ONE MAN

A lot of men begin affairs purely because they are bored and seek a little variety – a new woman with whom to make love. You can stay one jump ahead of the game by being all those different women: the flirt, the virgin, the mother, the temptress, the comforter, the wanton mistress, the romantic muse, the friend, and the confidante – all these and many more are possible. You may not find it easy to act a role that doesn't come naturally to you, but do be open to trying new approaches. It can be as liberating and fun for you as it is sexy for him.

Try to be all women to your lover – a little role-playing brings variety into the bedroom.

The Virgin

The Flirt

The Temptress

The Wanton Mistress

The Mother

DOS

Do communicate and compromise.

Do be assertive about your own wants
and needs.

✓

Do set boundaries and stick to them.

✓

Do help your partner find his sexual heaven.

DON'TS

Don't make your partner feel
awkward about asking for sexual activities.

✗

Don't say no without thinking about it.

✗

Don't become complacent
or let sex become a habit.

✗

Don't be afraid of being raunchy, seductive, or
suggestive if that's what your partner wants.

HOW TO REFUSE SEX
without causing a sulk

We all get turned off of the idea of sex from time to time – it would be unrealistic if we never expected to. In any good relationship knowing that one or other of the partners will, at some time, be unresponsive sexually is useful preparation for when it happens. If you have the sort of man who is caring and understands then you don't have a problem. If, however, you have the sort of man who expects you to be sexually active all the time and sulks if you refuse, then you have to be a little cautious in how you turn him down.

BEING HONEST

The key factors here are trust and respect. If you are in a good loving relationship it should be easy to reject a partner without causing offense – as easy as it would be to come on to them. Trust and respect means not lying to your partner and not making excuses. You should tell the truth; that you simply don't feel like sex – but you should also be aware that he has sexual needs and just because you don't feel like it doesn't mean to say that he can turn off his sexual tap and go without. If you were on a diet or not feeling hungry you wouldn't expect your partner to have to go without food just because you didn't want any, would you?

So turn down sex sometimes by all means, but make sure you offer your partner an appealing alternative. Perhaps you are too tired for full sex but you are happy to fool around a little, indulge in some mutual masturbation, or even just let your partner masturbate while he lies by your side and you caress him.

Just because you're not in the mood doesn't mean that he has to go without.

Try to reject your partner kindly and without causing offense – offer a little intimate consolation in place of full sex.

MEN ARE EMOTIONAL TOO

You have to realize that by saying no to your partner you are in fact rejecting him, no matter how skillfully or sensitively you do it. He, like you, is an emotional being who will feel rejected even if you are saying no just for the moment, rather than "You just don't turn me on and I'm not in love with you any more" – that might be exactly how he interprets your turning him down. By offering an alternative, such as masturbation, you are reassuring him that he is still loved, still wanted, and still desirable. By just saying no you are inadvertently reinforcing his belief that he is unloved and unwanted.

SAYING NO

Laying the groundwork is important. If you can see your partner getting ready for sex – perhaps running a soothing bath, getting dressed up (or undressed), pampering and preening himself – then it makes sense to signal that his efforts may be in vain long before he actually asks for or suggests sex. It saves him a lot of effort, and you the possibility of a sulk, but you should still try to offer an alternative. Saying "no" is fine, but saying "no, but perhaps tomorrow evening," or "save it for later," may be more productive for your overall relationship. Remember that in any sexual matter rejection is fraught with danger and has to be handled with care.

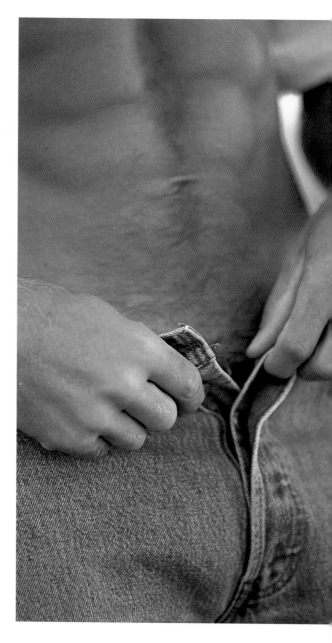

Men need to be loved and wanted but in different ways – always be careful of their feelings.

Dos

Do be kind to your partner
when turning down his advances.

✓

Do offer an alternative, no matter
how basic or simple it may be.

✓

Do be considerate of his sexual needs.

✓

Do explain that saying no to sex
isn't saying no to him as a person or a lover.

✓

Do examine your motives carefully
when rejecting your partner's sexual advances.

Don'ts

Don't make excuses.

✗

Don't lie or be uncommunicative.

✗

Don't forget that sex is an important part of any
relationship, and any long-term low libido needs
to be addressed.

✗

Don't reject your partner's advances in an
offhand or brusque manner.

✗

Don't forget that he has sexual needs too – they
may be quite different from yours but are
nevertheless just as valid.

WHAT EVERY
woman should wear in bed

You need to be warm in bed during the winter and comfortable at all times. However, you must remember when planning what to wear that you are going to bed with your lover. And that means making an effort every night if you want to keep your relationship alive and sparkling. Wearing your longest wooly nightgown may be both warm and comfortable – but is it sexy? You might feel that you do not need it to be sexy because you might not be getting ready for sex this evening. However, you are laying the groundwork for future sexual occasions and the long nightgown doesn't give off a good message to your partner. Whatever you wore on that first date is fine.

What you wear in bed is important. Making an effort for your lover shows that you care.

We all like to look and feel good and should be appreciative of the fact that our lover likes us also to look and feel good. What you wear in bed when you sleep alone is entirely your own business but, once you pull back the covers and invite another person into your bed, you have certain standards to keep up if you want the relationship to prosper.

TRACKSUITS AND FLANNEL NIGHTIES

This doesn't mean you have to go to bed wearing flimsy lingerie, or dressed in your partner's favorite nightwear every night. It simply means not letting your lover see you at your worst so if you are cold find something that will keep you warm but also give the right signals to your man. Sliding between the sheets completely nude must be preferable to wearing your granny's cast-off 1920s flannel nightie or some tracksuit that you find fabulously comfortable but is definitely not sexy.

A lot of women cover themselves up in bed not so much for warmth but because they have less self-esteem about their bodies than they deserve. Remember that your lover loves, wants, and desires you as you are. He will be flattered and pleased if you feel safe and comfortable enough to go to bed totally naked occasionally.

It might have been sexy for your grandmother . . . but times have changed – and so has underwear!

NAKED, SEXY, WARM, AND LOVING

In the bathroom you can use hair equipment such as curlers and combs as often as you want – but the bathroom is the place for them, not the bedroom. Likewise with face packs and creams, makeup removers, facial hair removers, acne creams, and anything else you may use.

When you are in bed with your lover, you should concentrate on that and nothing else. If you want to wear something in bed make sure it passes certain criteria – it must be sexy, revealing, concealing, and exciting. If the weather is cold why not try turning the heating up rather than your

dress sense down? Even if you're the hard-working mother of little children and a full-time professional you can still make an effort to be naked, sexy, warm, and loving.

DYNAMITE IN BED

Knowing what nightwear your lover likes the most is the best love aid you could ever have – wear it (whatever it is) when he is least expecting it and the result will be explosive. Don't complain if it is not something you would have chosen, you are pleasing your lover and what could be more important than that? You should only say something to him if what he has chosen is uncomfortable for you physically, or if you find it really too bizarre to wear. Then you will both have to compromise.

If you really want dynamite why not try wearing his fantasy nightwear not in bed, but when you are out with him for the evening. You could hide it discreetly under a long coat or under whatever outfit you have chosen to wear. The important thing is to let him have a little glimpse at some unexpected moment – and then see what happens! Be prepared for fireworks.

Know what your partner likes you to wear in bed. If you are pleasing your lover, you are really making love.

Dos

Do make an effort – you are sleeping
with your lover, not an old friend.

✓

Do try to be as sexy as possible at all times.

✓

Do occasionally go to bed wearing whatever
is his personal sexual fantasy (but don't
expect much sleep).

✓

Do set yourself standards and stick to them.

Don'ts

Don't wear anything if the alternative is not sexy.

✗

Don't treat the bedroom like
an extension of the bathroom.

✗

Don't be frightened of your own nudity or your
own body – be proud and flaunt what you've
got.

✗

Don't wear anything your granny would!

THE PLEASURE OF
mutual masturbation

Mutual masturbation can create a richer sexual life because it gives both of you the opportunity to experiment with what brings the most pleasure without the pressure of performing or having to have full penetrative sex. Each of you can enjoy yourselves and your orgasm without having to do too much yourself – perfect pleasure.

SETTING THE SCENE

You can set the scene with soft lights, romantic music and, if you both are happy to include it, an erotic video. If you like, use lubrication such as baby oil on the penis or the vulva. There is a range of positions for mutual masturbation. The only practical requirement is for both of your genitals to be within easy reach. And for you both to want to.

You could both lie side by side, with your upper body resting on your partner's. You can both then easily reach the other's genital area and he can kiss your face and neck and stroke your hair. At the same time your partner can feel your breasts with his hands. One of your hands is free to guide his toward doing what you like best and the other can reach toward his body and stimulate his penis and testicles.

AN EXCITING OPTION

Mutual masturbation is an alternative to penetrative sex and can add interest to a couple's sex life. It is also a great alternative when a man cannot get an erection; or a woman is pregnant, has just had a baby, or some recent surgery; or simply if either of the couple is tired. Many people just enjoy non-penetrative sex as an exciting sexual option. The etiquette of mutual masturbation is deciding on who comes first, and what happens afterward. Sometimes one partner might like to come and then go right to sleep. This is fine as long as the other partner is not feeling left out or frustrated. Perhaps this option could take place over two evenings so each partner gets a turn. And try not to make it into a race – although seeing who can come first might be an interesting variation occasionally. And who can hold off the longest. You can try anything.

Mutual masturbation increases your sex life tremendously.

DOS

Do try mutual masturbation if you are
both tired.

✓

Do concentrate on each other's orgasm.

DON'TS

Don't think of masturbation as being less than
sex – it's merely a different type of sex and is just
as valid and satisfying.

✗

Don't be selfish – make
sure you are both satisfied.

YOUR
masturbation

Not everyone wants to masturbate in front of their partner, but if you or he would like you to, why not try it since it can be a very rewarding experience? For you to be able to masturbate freely and enjoyably in front of your partner you have to feel safe and in a trusting relationship. Obviously your partner is crucial to this, but you can also help put yourself at ease by understanding and being familiar with your own aroused body.

Invite your partner to explore every inch of you while you pleasure yourself.

Take into consideration the fact that your partner may not know his way around your body as well as you do. He may well be nervous of exploring you, and you will be helping him learn more about you when you masturbate in front of him.

A GUIDED TOUR

Men's genitals are very much on show but yours are more hidden and secretive. Your partner may need a guided tour and lots of help in finding out how your genitalia work. It can be very sexy and exciting to show your partner exactly how to give you an orgasm by doing it yourself the first time for him. And on subsequent occasions he may feel flattered and excited if you masturbate in front of him. This is entirely a personal preference, so do ensure that you talk about it first. Some men do not like women to masturbate in front of them so if you are keen to add this to your sexual repetoire, you may have to encourage your partner to enjoy this particular aspect of your sexuality. You could

also suggest that he joins in while you are masturbating – helping you by rubbing your breast and nipples or inserting his fingers into your vagina as you come.

YOUR FANTASIES

If you want to share your fantasies with your partner that's fine but you have to be very very careful when it comes to revealing them. He may feel threatened or insecure by what goes on in your head. Telling him all your fantasies about him is fine but telling him that you imagine being ravished by twelve men in public may cause your lover to see you in a different light.

On the other hand, he may be extremely turned on. Only you can judge just how far it is appropriate to go. You can always find out what his favorite fantasies are and perhaps tailor yours to his in order to excite him even more. You can then get him to whisper fantasies in your ear as you masturbate yourself.

Dos

Do reassure your partner and let him explore
your body and find out how it all works.

✓

Do be free in front of him and avoid shyness.

✓

Do encourage him to help.

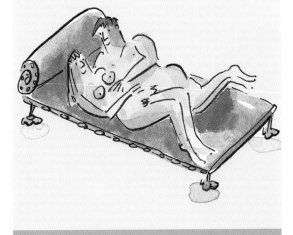

Don'ts

Don't let him think you've done this with other
partners even if you both know you have.

✗

Don't share any secret fantasies you may have
while masturbating – keep them to yourself.

hygiene

In China, whenever someone goes to the lavatory they run the taps in the sink to make some noise so that no one can overhear the sounds they make when they urinate or defecate. We might not go to quite the same lengths but there are still certain parameters regarding personal hygiene and etiquette that we should consider, even when we have lived with someone for a long time.

Maintain personal hygiene at all times. Feeling clean and fresh for your lover will increase your sexual confidence.

As human beings we make smells and noises, lose bits of skin and hair, have pimples and blackheads, and sweat from time to time. How much of this should your lover be subjected to? If you want your relationship to thrive, probably very little, but it is obviously up to you to decide what you are both happy with. If in doubt, try asking.

WHAT DO YOU DO?

By keeping your bodily functions to yourself you can retain an air of mystery and charm that will benefit your relationship and provide a certain respect and delicacy. By moderating your behavior the sense of sexiness and allure that you had when you were first seduced or courted can be kept alive. Remember that first date . . .

Personal hygiene covers a vast range of subjects from your verbal language (how you refer to sex, genitalia, and basic bodily functions), to your habits, from your dress sense, to your sleeping patterns. This means

Invest in the very best personal hygiene products – but tidy up any mess afterward.

that it's a matter of what you sleep in as much as how you pass water. Maintaining standards isn't difficult and doesn't negate you in any way. By doing it, you are expressing respect for your lover, emphasizing how important they are to you, and demonstrating to the world at large that you care about yourself intensely – and that's a good thing.

SETTING THE STANDARDS

Before you can begin to maintain your hygiene standards you have to set them. In order to do this, you have to look very closely at yourself as you are now. You have to know what your bad habits are, to see how far you have let yourself slip from the ideal your lover first met. Ask him what

Being clean and fresh for your lover is important and sexy.

annoys or embarrasses him about your personal hygiene and address it immediately. All men are different, were brought up differently, and have differing levels of interest in their lover's personal habits. Only you can decide and know what is right for them – and for you as a couple.

All these things need to be looked at and changed if they are upsetting. For instance when you first met your lover, you probably took lots of time over your appearance, because you wanted to look your very best. Do you still take that time? And do you still make that effort? If not, why not?

ERODING PERSONAL SPACE

When you first met your lover you wouldn't have dreamed of picking pimples in front of him; of not shaving your armpits; of wearing old flannel pajamas to bed; or of passing gas, burping, picking your nose, or changing your tampon in front of him. So what happens? A few years down the line and into a relationship we all find ourselves doing these things and thinking nothing of them. The personal space gets eroded and we let standards slip. Go back to basics and re-establish your ground rules, reinvent your private self, and rediscover your allure and privacy. Maintaining standards is good etiquette.

Standards obviously vary and that is okay – the question is, what bothers your partner? How much is acceptable, or unacceptable, to him? For some men there is nothing you can do that will shock or surprise them – you just need to

ask your partner to find out what sort of man he is. If you do feel he would rather not be exposed to all your hygiene routines, try to rearrange them so that you become the person your lover first fell in love with again. You will notice the difference this makes to your relationship.

You both deserve the best – it is important for long-term partners to maintain standards.

Dos

Do set and maintain standards.

✓

Do present the clean and hygienic side of
yourself but do the routine in private if that is
what your partner prefers.

✓

Do be aware of your lover's
feelings and sensitivities.

Don'ts

Don't carry out body maintenance in front of
your partner if he doesn't like it.

✗

Don't use the bedroom as a bathroom.

✗

Don't let your personal standards slip.

MENSTRUATION AND
your sex life

Purely because they are so alien to them, there aren't many men who fully understand or empathize with women's monthly cycles. They aren't being unhelpful or disrespectful on purpose. It may seem that your partner does not offer as much support and sympathy during your period as you would want but this is probably not because of indifference, rather

Women's cycles can be a mystery to men. Help him to understand what you are going through.

it is down to biological differences. Men simply have no experience of what it is like to menstruate.

A DEMURE APPROACH

Once you appreciate that your partner's possible sensitivities regarding this "strange" and taboo area are fraught and raw, you may feel more forgiving and less confrontational. No matter how "new age" your man might be he may still find the sight of you changing your tampon in front of him eerily shocking. However, your man may be one of the few who has no problems with this, and he is understanding, sympathetic, and interested – lucky you! But whatever type of man he is, perhaps a slightly more demure approach may be beneficial, purely because you are in a relationship with someone who, to all intents and purposes, might as well be a different species. But none of this is set in stone and only you will know how your lover reacts and what he finds off-putting.

The same goes for the disposing of tampons or sanitary pads – and for buying them. No matter how brave or confident your man might be this is

still an area that is intensely female and private and one he may never quite get right. Nothing is more daunting for a man than to be confronted with lots of shelves stocked high with sanitary wear that is confusing and unknown. They don't have the right life experiences to make the right choices so make sure, if your partner is happy to buy them, that you give him clear instructions as to what type you use.

MYSTERIES AND CLOSED BOOKS

Appreciating the fact that your lover is not as knowledgeable about your menstrual cycle or as sympathetic as you would like will hopefully relieve you of a lot of the frustration that can occur. The same goes for PMS (premenstrual syndrome) and its associated symptoms, which can range from destructive violence, aggression, fatigue, bloating, and headaches to a general feeling of

A demure approach may be beneficial. Your partner may not want your period details thrust in his face.

lethargy, and a lower or higher than normal interest in sex. Men don't have PMS so it will always remain a mystery and a closed book to them. You can elicit your partner's support and sympathy but deep down he may never really understand. However, it is good manners on his part to try and learn more about your cycles, and he should definitely make allowances, be more supportive during this time, appreciate you don't feel at your best, and generally stay out of the way or be warmer – so make sure you tell him.

It is best to appreciate that your partner will never fully understand your monthly cycles rather than confronting him about them and making him pretend to be as supportive as you would like. A good relationship is built as much on respect and understanding the differences as trying to be equal and modern. Give your partner the space to be unsure of himself in this delicate area and perhaps he will be more supportive as a result. Miracles do happen! Men aren't uncaring about this – merely unknowing – so educate them.

Your partner will be supportive if he understands more. Educate him sensitively about your cycle.

Dos

Do let your partner be unsure
of himself without getting angry.

✓

Do appreciate that men
don't have this life experience.

✓

Do be circumspect in your behavior in this area.

✓

Do be prepared to dispose of used tampons
and pads in private if your lover finds them
embarrassing.

✓

Do warn your partner when you
have PMS rather than expecting him to guess.

Don'ts

Don't make him buy your
sanitary wear just to prove a point.

✗

Don't change your tampon in front
of him if he would prefer you didn't.

✗

Don't leave packets of tampons lying around –
keep them private if that is his preference.

✗

Don't confront your partner.

✗

Don't expect total understanding.

BEING
raunchy

We all have more than one side to our personality. Sometimes we like to be demure and well behaved, and sometimes we like to swing from a chandelier, express our wild side, and have raunchy sex. The trouble is that for a lot of us our upbringing makes us reluctant to go for the wildness, in case it's seen as somehow wrong, in poor taste, or even sinful. So when you want raunchy sex you might well feel inhibited about asking for it or expressing how you feel. There is a certain etiquette about expressing your sexual needs that should help to overcome these inhibitions.

BEING WILD WITH WHIPPED CREAM

Obviously we all need to be wild at times but how do you ask to be tied up, or to have whipped cream spread over your nipples, or to have some fun with sex toys? What makes for good bedroom manners will depend on many things, including how safe you feel with your partner. Once you do feel safe you should be able to ask for pretty much anything you want without the fear of being rejected or made to feel dirty. Exploring the darker side of your sexual fantasies with your lover is fine. Acting out some of the more bizarre aspects of those fantasies might not be. Again compromise is the key word. You might, for example, harbor fantasies about being made love to by more than one man at a time. However your lover may well feel threatened by such a suggestion. The compromise might be to stick

Be a wild, raunchy woman if you want to be.

with one lover and use a vibrator as well – he can then have penetrative sex with you or you could perform oral sex on him while he pleasures you with the vibrator.

Likewise you may have fantasies about being tied up and soundly spanked, but your partner might feel intimidated by inflicting any sort of pain on you. You could try getting him to tie you up and then you compromise on the spanking part by using a feather whip or some other harmless whipping or spanking toy to simulate the pain aspect. Bring him around slowly.

Whatever you want is fine – just go for it. – as long as you're both comfortable with the experience.

DARK FANTASIES

We all have dark fantasies and knowing how to get them played out is an important part of a sexual relationship. You shouldn't be coy and shouldn't allow your fantasies to go unexpressed throughout your life because you are scared of what your partner might think. Talk to him about this. He will also have a dark side that needs expressing – perhaps you will be able to realize your fantasies together.

The etiquette of being raunchy is first to accept that you have a wild side and that it is both healthy and beneficial to express it. Secondly it is better to explore your sexuality within the loving and safe boundaries of a supportive relationship than in one-night stands or unsatisfying casual sex that may be both unhygienic and unsafe. Be prepared to compromise on all aspects of sexual matters but do express your wants and needs in trust and safety.

AVOIDING CONFRONTATION AND CONFUSION

As the world changes for the better in its treatment of women, more and more females are beginning to find and express their sexuality in a very real and physical way. For some men this can be difficult if they have been brought up to think that a woman's sexuality is less aggressive than their own. Obviously there is a need for some education in these cases to bring your man up to the correct viewpoint. But this should be done gradually and kindly to avoid confrontation and confusion.

Once you've got your partner open to the idea that you enjoy and want just as much raunchy sex as he does then you'll have a willing and very happy partner. It may take time, but it will be worth it.

Expressing your sexuality within an established, loving relationship is best.

Dos

Do express your wilder side sexually.

✓

Do try to get your partner's
cooperation and help.

✓

Do explore your sexuality within the safe
parameters of a loving relationship.

✓

Do be prepared to give as much as you receive.

Don'ts

Don't bottle up your darker side.

✗

Don't look for expression in casual sex.

✗

Don't frighten or shock your lover – be tactful
and discreet in your expression of your needs,
particularly initially.

THE ART OF
lovemaking

Adam and Eve could get away with it in public. But they were the only two people on Earth!

Lovemaking is such a close, personal, intimate activity that there has to be certain guidelines and boundaries set so that you both, as a couple, know where you are and can relax and have more fun. To begin with, if one of you wants to have sex and the other doesn't, for whatever reason, then the one who doesn't has right of veto. It's as simple as that. If you do not want to, you do not have to.

There should be no pressure put on you to do so, nor should there be any sulking (*see pages 18–19*) or bad temper. It's your body and you can decide at any time what you want to do with it. This also goes for the style, frequency, intensity, and location of any sexual activity. You have to be a full and willing participant for it to be loving sex.

GROWN-UP SEX

How, when, and where you have sex are all bound up with good etiquette. For instance, you shouldn't have sex in public places where you can be seen. It is bad manners to shock or offend anyone else with your sexuality. Nor should you have sex in front of your children or friends. A certain discretion and decorum is required of you and, naturally, you should be happy with this as a consenting and mature grown-up. It's possible that when we are a little younger, and a little more headstrong, we need a few more reminders that it simply isn't socially acceptable to display lust in public. And bear in mind that it may well be against the federal laws in your state.

Displaying affection in public is fine, just make sure that you take others into consideration.

KEEPING THE NOISE DOWN

It is considered good etiquette to keep the noise down when you are making love if you know you can be overheard. You would think this is obvious, but it is surprising how many neighbors complain about couples nearby being far too energetic in their passion. Try and be considerate at all times.

Your neighbors may complain if your lovemaking is too noisy. Be considerate.

YOUR RIGHTS

As a woman you have the right to be adored, worshiped, and seduced by your lover. You have the right not to be abused, hurried, or taken for granted. In order to exercise your rights you may need to communicate your wants and needs – and communicate them clearly, and, at times, possibly forcefully. Be assertive about your sexual preferences and don't ever accept second best.

GOOD TASTE AND DECENCY

Having considered your children, friends and relatives, and the neighbors, you should also consider each other not only as a couple but also as friends. Some couples seem to treat each other worse than they would treat a casual acquaintance. Your lover should also be your best friend, and as such is entitled to esteem, courtesy, and good manners at all times. And you should also be able to expect this from them. This means you must approach lovemaking with a degree of respect. This doesn't have to make it all serious, merely well mannered. For instance whatever your partner wants, sexually, should be considered and they, in return, should consider your wants and

needs. It's simply bad manners to concentrate entirely on your own sexual requirements while failing to address your partner's. You need to be accommodating – within certain boundaries of good taste and decency of course – but, apart from that, whatever he wants should be tried. And of course whatever you want is also allowable. He may want raunchy sex and you gentle intimate lovemaking – you just need a little compromise here for you to both achieve what it is that you want.

MAKING IT THE BEST

Although your own orgasms are important it is also vital that you give as much pleasure as you receive. As a woman, you may be capable of multiple orgasms but chances are, unless he's studied tantric techniques, your lover won't be. He may only get the one and so you have to make it the very best for him. And don't neglect the psychological aspect of sex for men. Not only does your partner want to come but he also needs to be satisfied visually and emotionally, sensuously and completely – a holistic experience that transcends the mere physicality of sex. You have to provide the complete package just as he has to for you.

Make it the best for each other. Giving as well as receiving makes the experience more satisfying.

Dos

Do have respect for your neighbors,
children, and friends.

✓

Do treat your lover like your best friend.

✓

Do be bold enough to experiment.

✓

Do treat lovemaking with respect and decorum
but not too seriously, have fun.

Don'ts

Don't accept second best
when it comes to lovemaking.

✗

Don't negate your lover's sexual needs
and wants.

✗

Don't do anything you don't want to – and don't
allow yourself to be pressured into doing so.

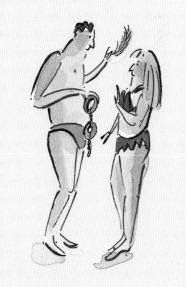

index

acknowledgments

Hulton Getty: 102
The Image Bank: /Color Day Productions 69, /Britt Erlanson 51, /Erlanson Productions 42.
Stockmarket: /Nancy Brown 115.

Tony Stone Images: /Bruce Ayres 22b, 32, /Donna Day 19, /Dale Durfee 16, 100, /David Hanover 22t, 48, /David Harper 12, /Chris Harvey 122, /Linnea Lenkus 58, /John Millar 18, /Laurence Monneret 77, /Ken Scott 111.